STUDENT SUCCESS STORIES

Jonathan Sprinkles & Friends

To:_____

From:_____

**Our greatest glory is not in never failing,
but in rising up every time we fail.**
- Ralph Waldo Emerson

ISBN 0-9726042-1-9

Printed in the United States of America

This book is available for quantity discounts for bulk purchases.

Credits
Cover design by HSA Design, 212-575-5091
Copyediting by Pryce Editorial Consultants, 817-774-0164
Book layout by Jonathan Sprinkles
Published by Instruments of Peace

.

Table of Contents

Dedication

*With love and enthusiasm, we dedicate this book
to all students, past, present and future.
We believe in you!*

Introduction

Okay, okay. I'll come clean. When I initiated this project, I had no clue what I was getting myself into. Just after I finished the final draft of my first book *Why Settle? Be the Best YOU That YOU Can Be*, I called my friend James Malinchak to update him with my progress. "Congratulations with taking the first step in becoming an author, Jonathan," he said. "So, what's the title?" When I told him, he got quiet for a second then replied, "Hmm, sounds good, but it doesn't tell me who you're speaking to. It doesn't give me a good idea of who your target market is. If you spoke to polar bear trainers from Iceland, you would need a book that says 'polar bear trainers from Iceland' in the title. If you're looking to attract more business in the high school and college markets, you will have to have a book with the word 'student' in the title. Don't make your audience guess who you are."

Makes sense, I figured. My mind immediately began to move 100 miles per hour. I felt that the book that I had worked so hard on wasn't good enough. I needed to do better—quickly! I tossed around tons of ideas that would give me a quick product with the right title on the front. In a way, I focused more on the cover than I did the actual content. Hey, I'm just keeping it real.

"Success Tips for Super Students" was the name that I came up with. Yes, it was cheesy, but it had that magical word "students" in it, so I could get over it. It was going to be a book filled with clever quotes from famous dead people. Yeah! That was it. I could finish the entire project in two weeks. In my eyes, it was a slam dunk.

As fate would have it, just before I started the book, I wrote a story that talked about the worst time in my life. It occurred during my junior year in college and almost prevented me from hanging around for my senior year. Interestingly, it was also what I consider to be one of the defining moments of my life. Even today, I look back on that situation as *"proof"* that I have the mental toughness to take whatever life throws my way. What felt like a curse at the time ended up being one of my life's greatest blessings. I no longer have questions about whether I can make it or not. If I did it once, I know I can do it again, come what may.

As I shared this story during speeches and workshops, I listened to other students who had similar defining moments in their lives. Their trials were producing powerful declarations of unshakable faith in their lives as well. Then it hit me, I didn't need to look very far at all in order to get the material for another book. There was enough material on the campuses of America's learning institutions to write volumes of student success books. Even more so, there were former students who would also have powerful stories to share. We can all relate to being a student at some point in our lives. This book would be relevant to a market that extends much further than just those that are currently in school.

I sent out queries across the country- asking for people who felt that they had a story to share with others to submit for this book. As I began to receive submissions, I quickly realized that this book was going to be much greater in scope and depth than I could have ever imagined. The project was bigger than Jonathan Sprinkles. It was a divinely-ordered compilation of compelling testimonies meant to bring change in the lives of the thousands of people who would read it. My role was not to be an author, but a vessel for this book to come to pass. My former aspirations were quickly poured out in favor of humility and appreciation for being the one chosen to handle such an awesome task. I'm so glad that I saw the light between then and now.

As I sat in silence, reading line after tearful line of the stories, my jaw frequently dropped in disbelief. I even remember asking myself out loud, "Oh my goodness. I'm surprised that she didn't just give up. What kept her going?" I was continually amazed by the accounts of a relentless inner drive to overcome life's challenges.

Though there were several dominant themes, there are two components that every story possessed. Every person that made it through his or her test had two things: 1) a refusal to crumble under the pressures of life and 2) a clear vision for their future that extended beyond the current circumstances. I believe these to be the keys to all personal victories. When we decide that giving up is not an option, we are willing to go through hardships until we get to our destiny.

In the case of the students in this book, some fought for academic redemption, others fought for their lives. Without exception, none of them stopped fighting until they saw their plan come to fruition.

Then the light began to shine again. I connected the dots and saw the entire picture for what it was. In a time of materialism, overt sexuality, institutionalized racism and the countless other social ills that plague our nation, *Student Success Stories* is a beacon of hope and a recipe for victory. It is a positive step toward bridging the gaps in the lives of young people.

As you read through the stories, you too will see that though we all differ in socio-economic background, gender, and ethnicities, we all share painful experiences that shaped who we are today. We are united through our pains, insecurities, mistakes and problems. Our struggles proved us to be more alike than we were different. I am convinced that our problems were given to us so that we could share with others how to overcome adversity and thrive, no matter the circumstances. Yes, our pain had a purpose.

This book is meant to enlighten those who have gone astray and affirm those who are doing the right thing. Wherever this book finds you on your journey through life, please know that if we did it, you can to. We are no different than you are. As a matter of fact, you are at an advantage because you now have coaches in your corner that are cheering you on. You, my friend, are in the process of creating your own success story!

You can do it!

Jonathan Sprinkles & Friends

And I Almost Gave Up!
By Cheronda Simmons

Tuesday, August 6th- I was ten days away from receiving my MBA in E-Commerce. The word "enthusiastic" would not come close to describing how I felt about my big day. The invitations were sent out and the parties (yes, parties-plural) were planned. My family, who had financially prepared for my graduation day by saving up money months in advance, was also very excited about the occasion.

At 8:57 P.M., I logged onto my school's grade system. My fingers nervously typed to locate my final grade from a one-hour elective that I was taking. As I looked onto the screen, my vision became blurry as tears filled my eyes. I closed the program and opened it again to be sure that the system was retrieving the correct score. Again, the same grade stared back at me—a D. Oh my God! I knew what this meant. Graduation was no longer in my future because the MBA program does not allow students to graduate with a D on their report card.

Figuring that this had to be a mistake, I decided to inquire with the professor about my grade. The professor responded to my inquiry by informing me that my grade was calculated by considering only the paper that he assigned the class to write. I was dumbfounded when I discovered that the D in the course resulted from the D that he gave me for my final paper on employee retention policies. Ironically, I wrote the paper about the company that I am currently an employee of.

I was deeply insulted when he said to me that my writing was less than that of an undergraduate student. He continued to inform me that his frustration caused him to stop reading and give me my grade after reading only the first four pages of my 20-page paper. I tried to reason with him via email and asked for an opportunity to rewrite the entire paper, making changes where he thought it would be appropriate. I even informed him that I needed to pass this class to graduate. He was unwilling to work with me and advised me to appeal my grade to the Dean.

I stormed into the other room where my boyfriend was typing on his laptop. I fell into his arms, almost knocking the computer out of his lap. I was heartbroken. Crying uncontrollably, I was barely able to get out the choppy statement, "I am not going to graduate." He didn't understand what happened and asked me to calmly explain the scenario. I re-enacted the scenario for him and explained to him that I was told to appeal my grade. He dropped what he was doing and took on the challenge of writing my letter of appeal on the spot. "Less is more," he said. "Let's just keep it simple. We don't have to show all of our cards right now." I immediately submitted the appeal to the Dean.

Monday, August 12th- I checked my email first thing in the morning at 8:30 A.M, hoping to have received a response from my appeal. No such luck. This was only five days before graduation and four days before my family was scheduled to arrive. I had not slept through the night since the day that I had received the devastating news.

At approximately, 3:30 P.M., I received an email back from her that very stoically said, "Appeal denied."

Denied! What? I wasn't asking for an A in the course. I just wanted to graduate, get my diploma and be done with the program. Even a C would have been more than acceptable. Surely that wasn't too much to ask for considering the circumstances. I did not, in my wildest imagination, believe that she would deny my appeal. Not after I cited verbatim the rules in the student handbook as the basis of my defense. Ironically, she used these same rules as the basis of her denial.

In her letter, she said that if I was not satisfied, I could proceed with the appeal process by contacting the Vice President of the school. Of course I wasn't satisfied. I informed her that I refused to accept this response and that I would be continuing with the appeal process.

After submitting my letter to the Vice President of the school, I proceeded to inquire to the Dean about the possibility of participating in the graduation ceremony with the appeal decision pending. In essence, I would put on my cap and gown and walk across the stage, not knowing if I would really receive my degree or not.

She emailed me back and said something so astonishing that I will never forget it. She said, "You can participate in the graduation ceremony *and no one will ever know.*" How was I supposed to respond to a statement like this? Was I supposed to be satisfied with playing make-believe with my future? Was I to overlook the countless hours of studying and thousands of dollars worth of student loans that brought me to this point? I felt compelled to let her know my feelings. I typed a message responding to her, "This is not a true statement because God and I will know, but I will do my best to keep my head up while considering the circumstances. God Bless You!"

I was actually about to settle for being able to participate in the graduation ceremony and started to plan on taking classes for the fall semester. I even applied for financial aid. My spirits lifted, figuring that the consolation of walking (though I was not actually graduating) was better than the embarrassment that I would experience from having to tell my family and friends about what happened. Maybe the Dean was right, no one would ever know. Sure I was angry, but I was also in touch with reality. However, something burning on the inside of me refused to allow this situation to keep me from finishing the program.

I decided not to share my experience with anybody. On Monday, I would finalize all graduation plans and proceed with business as usual. I could not believe it, I was settling. I never settle! Nevertheless, on Tuesday night, I continued to pray. Even though my decision was already made, I prayed anhow. My prayer was that God would speak to the hearts of the decision makers. I never knew what kind of testimony this prayer would lead to. God never gives up, even when we give up, settle or turn our backs from Him in times of turmoil.

Wednesday, August 14th- Just three short days away from graduation, I received an unexpected email in my inbox. The e-mail came from my Dean. It said the following:

> "Cheronda, after going home yesterday and having time to really think about the situation, I have decided to change your grade. I will be submitting the change of grade to the Registrars Office today. Enjoy

the ceremonies on Saturday with peace of mind. If you decide to continue with the appeal process please let me know."

I could not believe it. God continued to work, even after I had given up. My prayers had been answered. It was a testimony reminiscent of the old saying "God may not come when you want him, but He is always on time." I responded to the Dean and informed her that I would accept her grade and would not continue with the appeal process. I thanked her for reconsidering my situation. I thanked God for never giving up on me even when I gave up on myself. I vowed to myself that I would never settle again.

Saturday, August 17th- At 11:30 A.M., I heard the sweetest words that I had ever heard, "Cheronda Simmons candidate for MBA in E-Commerce". They rang throughout the auditorium, mixed with cheers as I walked up the stairs to shake the Dean's hand. She smiled at me with great pleasure as she firmly shook my hand. I smiled back with re-assurance that she had made the correct decision. She and I were the only ones that knew the true meaning of that special moment.

The events that took place during the previous two weeks played in my head as I walked across the stage. I almost couldn't believe that I was there. I had been supporting myself with a full-time job while a full-time student. I was a black female who was the first in her family to go to college. Despite the pressure, despite the odds, despite even wanting to give up, I was achieving yet another milestone in my life. I made it! I am now Cheronda D. Simmons, MBA!

Designs of Success
By Jacqueline W. Ivey

"…success is to be measured not so much by the position that one has reached in life as by the obstacles which he has overcome while trying to succeed."
                                        -Booker T. Washington

Circumstances are not always exactly what we would desire for them to be. There is always someone worse off than we are, and yet we all sometimes feel helpless in regards bettering our situation. We even believe that we cannot do any better than where we are, so we settle for doing just enough to get by or use the excuse that because we are at a "disadvantage", we cannot do any better.

Having grown up as the youngest of five children in a small, rural South Carolina town, there were not many opportunities to better myself. I could have just accepted my circumstances and settled for what was available to me. Instead, I chose to use my "disadvantages" as steppingstones to set goals for myself and to strive to achieve them. After all, we are our own *change agent*. I have learned that many people cannot look past their disadvantages to see the vast sea of opportunity that is available to them if they would apply themselves.

I recently interviewed a young woman to whom I asked, "What motivates you?" She replied, "Life." I wholeheartedly agreed with her, for I've always believed that the greatest motivation is being alive to experience new things each new day, appreciating the gifts, talents, and abilities that I've been given while putting them to use daily.

My drive to succeed developed very early in my life. My family was not wealthy, and I was considered to be "at-risk" because of the socio-economic makeup of my family and the community in which I grew up. Neither of my parents ever completed a grade-school education. My father was a laborer and my mother was a "domestic engineer" in other people's houses. However, these two individuals were the most intelligent and well-educated people that I knew, because they both had a *B. L. Degree* (Bachelor of Life).

My parents were very firm to put it mildly. I often considered them to be the most insane people on the face of the earth. I'm sure that I was not the only child to ever think that about their parents. My parents had very high, mostly unspoken expectations of what they hoped each of their five children would accomplish. For as long as I can remember, my father always imparted this simple admonition, "Keep your mouth shut, your eyes and your ears open." By merely following this small piece of advice, have I gained a wealth of knowledge throughout my life.

My mother, who died as a result of congestive heart failure 18 months after I moved back home after graduating from college, was a very strong woman to whom life had dealt a number of unfair blows. She taught me about integrity. She was a woman who believed in fairness and was always willing to speak up for what was right, even if it made her unpopular.

Kingstree, South Carolina was the last place that I wanted to be with my degree in hand, new-found independence, but I am thankful that I had the opportunity to be there with my mother for that difficult period. Toward the end of her life, I learned quite a few things from her about cooking, spirituality, and faith.

In addition to my parents, I have been fortunate enough to encounter a multitude of people who have influenced various stages of my personal growth. The small community that we called "Rock Town" is considered "the wrong side of the tracks" by most. It consists of working class folks who were not wealthy materially, but who were rich in family and a sense of community, (though we too had the usual neighborly squabbles). People looked out and cared for one another.

The neighborhood was filled with like Mr. Buck, who went out of his way and made several trips back and forth on Sunday morning , just to make sure that his family and many of his neighbors had a ride to church. His wife, Mrs. Shing, cooked at the elementary school. Because most of us were on "free lunch", we got all of our meals from the cafeteria versus making them at home. All the neighborhood kids spoke to her as she placed the special of the day on our lunch trays. She was the model of humility, always operating in a pleasant demeanor. They said that she was capable of getting angry sometimes, but I honestly don't believe that she knew how to. Her commitment to being a cordial person was my first lesson in hospitality. Even today, when faced with trying circumstances, I ask myself, "What would Mrs. Shing do in this situation?"

There was also Mr. Jacob, a retired barber and Pentecostal minister, who sat on his porch and talked to us as we passed by his house on our way from the bus stop. "What did y'all children learn today in school?" he would ask. And we'd better be able to answer him! His wife Mrs. Liza, cared for half of the children in the neighborhood while our mothers worked.

Today, I draw encouragement from the thousands of students that I've had the pleasure of working with throughout South Carolina. Each of them with their individual personalities and innocence remind me of where I've been and where I'm going as I grow older. They remind me of how important it is to have child-like faith as I dream big, stay focused and strive for success.

The designs of our success are not just happenstance but are meticulously carved out by great designers in our lives through their words, examples, love, and support. The designers in my life were the motivators that drove me never to quit even when the assignments became hard. No matter what the circumstances are or where we come from, there are designs on our lives and designers waiting to help to coordinate ours success.

Finish the Race
By Jason Gipson

It's a sunny afternoon during the spring of my sophomore year in high school. My track coach has entered me in the open 400-meter sprint. This must be punishment for some sin that I committed unknowingly, because I hate the 400. Regardless if like it or not, our team needs points, so I'm running.

I set my blocks just right. Before backing into the blocks, I jump up and down a few times in an attempt to look like a real sprinter. I pray that I will glorify God through my running, and in return, I ask Him to not let me pass out and die on the backstretch.

I get set and wait for the gun. The gun sounds, and I take off. By the time I hit the first straightaway, I'm beginning to make up the stagger and I'm feeling great. We approach the 200-meter mark and I'm in position to take the lead. All of a sudden, I feel my right hamstring tighten up. I see my life flash before my eyes, and I see a long tunnel with a light at the end. Then, reality slaps me on the back of the head and tells me it's just a cramp. After two seconds of self-concocted drama, the rest of the field is passing me and I'm limping. As adrenaline and common sense kick in, I speed up and my leg loosens up. By now, there's no chance of winning, but I push myself and finish the race strong anyhow.

Four years later, I found myself at The University of Texas at Austin. I was a sophomore studying mechanical engineering. I began the Spring semester in the same manner that I had started the previous three semesters. I was on a mission to get an A in every class. My overall GPA was a 3.76, and I was determined to take it higher. The classes were getting more difficult, but I felt that I had academic momentum. I felt like running back Ricky Williams in the open field with nothing but a 180-pound cornerback standing between the goal line and me. It would take something serious to slow me down, but that is exactly what happened.

About two weeks into the semester, I got sick. I wasn't sure what I had, but I stayed in my dorm room for about a week. After dragging my sick body all the way across campus to the student health center, I walked out of the clinic with some useless antibiotics and no clue of what was ailing me. It got so bad that my mother drove up from Houston and took me home. I visited my doctor in Houston, and after about five minutes, he determined that I had infectious mononucleosis, better known as "mono." An analysis of my blood confirmed it. I stayed at home for another week before returning to school. Within two weeks I had lost 15 pounds.

When I started going back to class, looking like an urbanized version of death in jeans and sweatshirt, I realized that I was completely lost. I had missed tests, quizzes, labs and homework. My academic momentum was gone. Realizing that my semester was in shambles after only a month, I spoke with an academic counselor. She told me that my best option was a medical withdrawal. That meant that I would just have to pack up my things, go home, and try again next semester. So I said my goodbyes and headed for Houston.

After another couple of weeks under the care of "mommy," I was healthy--and bored. I had an offer to intern with Texaco during the summer, so I called them up and asked if I could start a little early. They gladly said yes, and I began working on St. Patrick's Day. Work kept me occupied, but I could feel the cobwebs starting to form in my brain. Internships are great for resumes, but they are not always intellectually stimulating. Making copies and playing Solitaire on the computer can only challenge you so much. I decided to take a history class at the local community college, so that I could at least make a little progress towards the completion of my degree.

At the end of the summer, renewed and refreshed from a long hiatus, I returned to school to conquer the engineering department. This was my intention, at least. My semester lineup was: Mechanics of Solids, Honors Thermodynamics, Fluid Mechanics, Materials Engineering, Technology and Current Social Issues. No sweat, right? Wrong.

The little history course I took during the summer did nothing to prepare me for the academic gauntlet that I was facing. I was rustier than Michael Jordan coming out of his last retirement. By the middle of the semester, I was just worried about passing all of my classes. I was sweating bullets during final exam week. By the grace of God, I did pass all of my classes, but my only A was in Technology and Current Social Issues, a one-hour class. I got a 'B' in one-hour lab, and the rest of my grades were all C's. Four C's? I didn't know what a C was before that semester. The damage to my ego was much bigger than the damage done to my GPA.

Over the winter break, I took time to focus and get my mind ready for the spring. While at home, I started thinking about how much I missed studying Spanish. When I started college, I wanted to double major in engineering and Spanish, but representatives from the engineering department told me that it was not allowed. Well, I really wanted to get back into Spanish, so I did what every child does when they don't get what they want. I went and asked someone else. I talked to the Spanish department, and they told me that there was nothing stopping me from getting a Spanish degree. Since my semester at home already set me back, I decided that I had nothing to lose. That spring semester, I enrolled in Spanish phonetics in addition to Kinematics and Dynamics, Thermodynamics II, Engineering Economics, and Honors Matrices. My academic momentum was building and I was almost feeling like Ricky again. I took one Spanish class a semester for the next three semesters. Instead of adding stress, my Spanish classes gave me the academic balance that I sorely needed. I took two Spanish classes during each semester of my fifth year and completed both degrees with an overall GPA above 3.5.

College has been one of the greatest experiences in my life thus far. It is much more important than my 400-meter experience in high school, but the lesson is the same. Sometimes, life throws you an obstacle that knocks you off course. Though you did not ask for them, and you may have done nothing to cause them, but the obstacles come nevertheless. The true test of your character is how you respond. Do you just quit and give up running altogether, or do you get back up and head for the finish line? Reassess your definition of winning, get up, and keep running for the finish line. As it has often been said, a setback is just a setup for a comeback.

JOHNNY CAMPBELL

It's So Easy To Quit, So Hard Stick With It
By Johnny "Transition Man" Campbell

The year was 1989. I was in my sophomore year of college. I was a Big Ten college athlete and was preparing for my upcoming season when I learned my mother had suffered a massive stroke. My heart raced with fear and anxiety upon hearing the news and I left college to be with her. I learned from the doctor that she'd lost most of her motor skills, her ability to speak and was confined to bed.

This situation was so serious and so troubling to me I decided not to return to college. My mother was my rock, especially so, because my father had recently died from diabetes. Because I am an only child, she was all the family I had. She was the pillar that kept me stable during the storms I faced growing up. And now my whole world, and all the security I had ever known, was being taken away and I was powerless to stop it. I struggled to keep a positive attitude during the long weeks of her nursing care, my heart ached with the thought of losing her and I could not imagine going on without her.

One day as I sat by her bedside watching her, she looked into my eyes and it seemed as if she were speaking to my heart. Her message, as I understood it, was direct and to the point, "My son, you must return to school and fulfill the promise you made to your father and me--no matter what happens to your parents, you will finish college".

My mother knew that having a college degree was critical for my future success and without it, I could face a life of mediocrity. She understood that in everyone's life there was trouble, adversity and the loss of loved ones. But she also knew that a person must persevere and hold on to their vision — especially when times got hard and the world deals serious life-changing blows.

Although, my mother was dying, she reminded me that my vision and willingness to persevere would be the key to my success in life. She believed if I kept my vision, and persevered, I would survive even while those around me failed.

With great apprehension, I returned to school to complete my education. I am not saying that it was easy given my mother's medical condition, but I held to my vision and finished. From this experience, I learned that in life you must learn to see beyond your immediate circumstances or situation, you must hold on to your vision, and you must be willing to remain steadfast through the storm in order to achieve your ultimate goal.

I achieved my goal. I graduated from college. Two months later, my mother passed away. She held in her heart the vision of my graduation and she held onto life until I came to her bedside and told her "Mama I kept the promise — I am now a college graduate." My mother achieved her goal, and with a look of joy on her face she release herself from this world. She persevered!

The true key to sticking it out and being successful in life is all about "holding on to your vision and persevering" to the very end, no matter what. For if you do, your reward is sure to come.

I Don't See Why Not
By Jonathan Sprinkles

I wanted to cry but couldn't find the tears. I sat in my dorm room looking at the white brick walls wondering if I really would become another statistic. Many years of not applying myself so that I would fit in with the "cool" kids had more than caught up with me. They left me with some horrible study habits. I stared across the room at the computer screen displaying my semester's grades. I turned in three C's and a D. I'll do the math for you. I cringe as I say this –that was a 1.75 GPA.

For my entire life, I grew up fighting off the negative stereotypes that surround African American males. I heard that one out of every three black men was in jail or under the watch of the penal system. The media said that the average life expectancy of black males was 25, and that we were more likely to die at the hands of another black male than any other cause. The most blaring statistic was that there were more black men in jail than there were in college. For those who have never experienced such morbid expectations, it is impossible to understand how this made me feel about my heritage, my life and my future. It was almost as though I had been born to fail.

Though I tried to take on the weight of the world and change the perceptions through my attempts at success, I too became engulfed in a world of hurt. I had every opportunity to prove the world wrong, but my lack of focus had gotten the best of me. Here I was at one of the best colleges in the country, and I too was doomed to contribute to another negative statistic.

Everyone who has been to college knows that the most crucial years are your junior and senior years. In school, we were told that employers with a big heart would wink at our first two years if we performed during your last two. That wasn't my story. My classes were much tougher and the professors weren't playing.

I was already kicked out of my internship program for falling below a 3.0 GPA. Now I was in danger of losing the scholarship that took care of my tuition as well as my Resident Assistant position, that gave me free housing in the dorms. Though my cumulative GPA was not quite bad enough to get me kicked out of school, losing my financial backbone surely would have forced me to drop out.

While those on the outside looked at me and saw a positive, goal-oriented, well-known campus leader, my world inside was deteriorating quickly. I could literally feel the tension swelling in my shoulders as knots began to form. The front of my head pounded so hard that I clutched it tight, trying to make it stop. The pressure was mounting and I was less than an inch away from bursting.

Who could I turn to? Though it was bad enough that I was stranded all by myself with no hope, telling others would mean blatantly admitting my failure. I would have to endure the embarrassment of people saying, "You? How did you allow yourself to get in this position? I never thought that *you of all people* would be close to failing out." That was the last thing that I needed to hear. I was a proud young man, having worked hard for three years to earn a positive reputation. I took painstaking efforts to have people know that I was a "good man" who had his stuff together. Ironically, this public façade had its hands around my neck, choking the life out of me. I didn't feel like I could even turn to Jason, my roommate of three years. He was known for making 3.8's and above –in engineering classes no less. I was alienated by my failure. Should I stay and hide or should I just quit now? Maybe the stereotypes were true. Maybe I really *was* born to fail.

As I sat on the end of my bed, I made a list of all the reasons why I hated myself for getting into this situation. My self-confidence was completely gone. I felt like I was on my deathbed, preparing to write my obituary. Then, out of the dead silence, a still, small voice spoke to me and said, "That's enough." I wish I could say that I saw angels, stage lights, and background dancers, but it wasn't that deep. All that I heard was, "That's enough." It wasn't a mouthful, but I completely understood what it meant. All of a sudden, I knew that somehow things were going to work out. Just like a mother singing a sweet lullaby to soothe her crying child, I felt a warm comfort, knowing that I was being watched over. Everything was going to be alright. The turbulent waters of self-hatred, fear, and anger all subsided that instant. I experienced the sensation that some describe as "the peace that surpasses all understanding." Though on paper I was down for the count, I still had one last punch to throw. This one had to be a knock out! The tension eased, my spirits lifted and I prepared for the final round.

I began the process of reassembling the shattered mess called my academic career. I figured that in order to get what I never had, I needed to do what I had never done. Even if I didn't do any better, I certainly couldn't do any worse! I pinned up my goals for the semester and a calendar, mapping out every hour of my day. They were the first things that I saw in the morning and the last things at night. Like never before, I pursued success with a passion. Friday and Saturday, which used to be reserved for partying and sleeping in late, changed to study days. I visited each professor on a regular basis, making sure that they knew that I was interested in their class. Okay, sometimes *pretending* to be interested in their class. I ran my life like a business, priding myself on my newfound ability to plan and execute with precision.

Interestingly, my definition of "cool" also changed. My former years were marked by my efforts to be seen with the "in crowd." I freely exchanged being the person that I really was for the assumed personality that gave me social status. It was cool to me that I was viewed as a "leader's leader" that had no personal hang-ups, problems or insecurities of his own. After my conversion, however, all of that changed completely. I was only concerned with being known by the people that shared my passion for handling their business with the books. All the superficial stuff had to go.

When I opened my eyes, I saw students of all nationalities who wanted the same thing that I did – academic excellence. As I stopped shutting myself off from those who didn't look like me, the complexion of my friends went from all black to a beautiful array of ethnicities. As it turns out, we were much more alike than our perceived differences. Though our backgrounds varied, we united through our refusal to let any class make us settle for second best.

In my journey from tragedy to triumph, I learned a few things that changed my perspective about life:

what I do most is what I do best, what I focus on is what I see and what doesn't kill me will serve to make me stronger.

My mother always used to tell me, "What you do most is what you do best." I didn't know then, but I now understand what she meant. I pretended to be an inferior student for so long that I eventually became one. When I needed to dig deep to find the discipline to go to the next level, I quickly found that it was no longer in me to do so easily. Practice makes perfect, so I should have been more careful about what I was practicing.

I also realized that, for much of my life, I focused on the reasons why I *could not* succeed. Thus, my life became a product of the "why nots." When I changed my attitude and decided to focus on the reasons why I *could* win, breakthroughs began to happen. When I meditated on my fears, they consumed me. But as soon as I made a qualitative decision to close the door to the possibility of failure, the winner in me came alive. The side that I fed the most was the side that won the most. The one that I gave the power to is the one that got the victory.

Though quitting was always a viable option, poignant reminders of the sacrifices of generations past etched themselves in my mind. Those before me suffered through the torment of overt racism, fire hoses, even snarling dogs so that I could have a chance to compete at a major university. With that in mind, I erased the question of whether or not I would endure what had become the biggest challenge of my life.

The event that was created to bring my demise served to become my greatest source of strength. I now look back at that time and realize that if it didn't take me out, I was determined to walk away from it a stronger and more powerful man. If I found a way to survive, I could find a way to succeed. As long as I had one breath left in my body, I could use it to testify of God's grace.

The remainder of my college career became one for the record books. Going the extra mile would underscore my second shot at life. Like never before, I pursued success with a passion. I ran my life like a business, priding myself on my new-found ability to plan and execute with precision.

Making the Dean's List two of my final three semesters, I was kicking butt and taking names at the number five business school in the country. Yes! I looked at that thought of being a statistic and said, "Sure, I'll be a number—number one."

By the time I graduated, I was honored with the Barbara Jordan Leadership Award and inducted into the Dean's Dozen, a small group of students hand-picked by the Dean of Students out of an enrollment of over 50,000. Best of all, I was offered a sales job with one of the hottest companies in Corporate America at the time.

Scripture says that the steps of a good man are ordered by the Lord. Though the path doesn't always make sense, there is peace in knowing that it's all working together for the good. We were never promised that the road would be easy. All we know is that we won't ever walk alone.

I used to question why I had to go through so much pain and humiliation in order to arrive at a point where I finally believed in myself. But as I look back and see the determination and the testimony that my sufferings have produced, instead of asking "why," I now ask, "Why not?" What was the lowest point in my life produced a defining moment. My troubles may slow me down, but I refuse to let them stop me. Goodness and mercy have followed me all the days of my life. I have never walked alone, and I never will.

Pursue Your Dreams
By Jowanda Durham

Picture it—Georgia, 1996. The summer Olympics were in Atlanta. Heat and humidity was at a record high and I had just graduated from high school. Anyone who knew the Class of '96 in Middle Georgia, knew the cockiest eighteen year olds on the planet. I was no exception.

By June, I hadn't decided where I was going to attend college or what I would do when I got there. I was wavering between Mercer University, an extremely expensive private school and the number three party school in the nation, the University of Georgia. A year prior to graduation, I made the most important decision of my life. I accepted Jesus Christ as my Lord and Savior and I decided that I would not make frivolous decisions that weren't "led by God." I really wanted to be where God wanted me to be.

Mercer offered a small scholarship- but it did not put a dent in the $18,000 per year tuition, plus expenses. Then there was UGA, a beautiful campus with a population of over 30,000 students, two hours from home, and free tuition due to the HOPE Scholarship. An obvious no-brainer, right? Wrong. There were two problems: first, my older brother was at UGA which meant that I would be cheated out of a car. Secondly, my ex-boyfriend formerly known as "my first love," was also attending that school. So, I made a decision. Forget the car, and forget the ex. There were over 30,000 students, so I did not have to run into him. Therefore, I chose to be challenged, to grow, and to thrive in a diverse academic atmosphere.

Because I followed my passion, I was able to stick it out and complete my education. I am a success in motion. I accomplish goals, and when they're met, I set new ones. I used a three-step process that allowed me to successfully graduate from college in exactly four years!

Step 1- Follow my passion.

When I arrived at UGA, I was undecided about my major, but I knew my heart's desire was theatre. I was afraid to venture into drama because I feared my parents and friends' responses. At my all-black high school, my teachers stressed the importance of higher education. We were encouraged to pursue medicine, law, education, and other "notable occupations." I graduated in the top 2% of my class and was senior class president. However, I was not a brain. Unlike some of my "smart" classmates, I did not score a 1000 on my SAT's and Princeton never came knocking.

The option of studying drama was unheard of! I saw many of my peers choosing majors so that they could make money. I am not against that, but they hated what they were studying. I considered other majors like English and journalism, but when I contemplated those careers, I was bored. I knew that I was selling myself short. However, when I attended my first acting class, my heart pounded outside of my chest and I met each assignment with anticipation. Therefore, I bit the bullet, listened to God and followed my passion. While other people were studying calculus, and economics, I was in the library reading monologues, plays, and auditioning. I chose to associate with other people who followed their passions and they became positive influences in my life.

**Step 2-Surround myself with people who are honest,
      positive, and encourage me to fulfill my dreams.**
By my junior year, I had defended my career choice to
enough people.   My parents never discouraged me
because they never understood what I was doing. I will
never forget when I went home, one of my parents'
friends congratulated me for leading the college band.
Completely   confused,   I   asked   him   to   explain.
Apparently, my father told him that I was a drum major,
not a drama major (I laughed for months).

      I did encounter a few people who disagreed with
my choice for a major. One classmate told me that I was
wasting my time. He thought that a sharp black woman
should go to college and pursue a more traditional path
that would guarantee success.   I did not allow this
comment to defer my dream, because I had surrounded
myself with several people who uplifted me during
times of discouragement. Emily, one of my best friends
and my roommate, was an art major.   She was
absolutely brilliant in every subject including science
and math and she rarely scored less than a B. As an
artist, she preferred creating beautiful oil and charcoal
paintings.   She taught herself how to play the cello,
guitar, violin, and piano. She also edited every paper
that crept out of our household. My other roommate,
Stephanie was majoring in speech communications. Her
dream was to graduate from college, and attend
seminary, so that she could return to New York to
evangelize to youth in the ghettos.   Today, she is
enrolled in seminary and working as a youth advisor to
under-privileged teens. Then there was Barry, a full-time
student, athlete, and 4.0 genius.   After more than two
years as a biology major, he switched his to business.

He followed his passion and is currently happily working in a premiere business consulting firm.

Our apartment was filled with speakers, artists, actors, preachers, musicians, and geniuses. People came over to our apartment to escape from mundane schoolwork. We were modern day muses! However, we did not confuse following your passion with a 24/7 party. When we accepted our passion and decided to actively pursue our God-given dreams, we encountered challenges and delays before we saw any victories. There was a price to pay for achieving and succeeding.

Step 3-Endure storms.
I do not know any person in life who did not jump hurdles in order to win the race. My favorite bible story is about Joseph. Joseph was a dreamer! He envisioned himself as a ruler over many people. When he shared his vision, his brothers despised him. For the next 20 years, Joseph was enslaved, wrongfully accused, and imprisoned! He definitely was not off to a great start but Joseph believed God was the giver of dreams. He overcame every dreadful situation in his life by developing a positive mental attitude. Joseph was loyal and faithful—faithful to God and to those in authority. Finally, Joseph reached his destiny. He was only second in command to Pharaoh, and was the ruler of Egypt.

When I think of Joseph's story I am reminded that I can endure any trial while holding on to a promise from God. When you live a purpose-filled life you look forward to each day's challenges and blessings.

During my senior year, I suffered from tremendous stress and anxiety. My schedule was hectic! On top of taking a full load of classes, I had a part-time job, was in a play, and led a bible study for freshman girls. I also started preparing for life after college by sending out resumes to film companies, submitting writing samples to fellowship programs, and auditioning for grad school at NYU. I thought I was going to have a mental breakdown. I often started my day at 6:00 A.M. and would not return to my apartment until midnight. However, I did manage to maintain over a 3.0 GPA and I placed as a semi-finalist in a national writing contest.

After graduation, I was not accepted into NYU's acting and writing program, nor was I hired by any major studio in California. However, I was blessed with the opportunity to be an intern with an independent film company. I continue to write and act as well as develop and grow my own web-based business. I have silenced the critics and listened to God's voice. But most importantly, I am happy. As I follow my God-given dreams, I live a purposeful and adventurous life.

All I Need is a Chance
By Kevin Rome, Ph. D

Unfortunately, there are too many high school students who arrive at college with no clue as to what to expect and how to navigate the collegiate experience. I can remember arriving to college as a freshman with no place to live (the old "they messed up my paper work" story) and not having a clue about what my life would be like for the next five years. I can remember trying to register for classes and seeing that "STAFF" was listed next to several classes. I was so naive that I thought to myself, "This person named '*staff*' is teaching a lot of classes." What it really meant was that no specific person had been identified to teach the course or the selected instructor was one that students avoided. By registering for the course the student would not know which instructor would teach to course. Granted, I still registered for several classes taught by "staff."

I worked my way through college—from work-study, to fast food, and then several telemarketing jobs so I could have what I thought were the essentials (you know, nice clothes.) In the process, I accumulated many credit cards. Come to think of it, I had approximately12 credit cards at one time, and no job. You can imagine how that situation turned out. When I graduated from college, landed my first job and did not have the credit rating needed to finance a car despite having a steady income. There is nothing more humiliating than being told "no" when you apply for credit.

As an undergraduate, it took me several years to figure out what I wanted to do with my life, but once the decision was made, I was determined to reach my goal. I decided that I wanted to go to graduate school. I was a resident advisor in the dorms and I really enjoyed the position. My supervisor said that I had a knack for the position and recommended that I pursue a career in "student affairs." I hadn't even realized that the profession existed.

As I developed a clear vision for my life, I found it easier to focus on my academics. However, my lack of commitment to academics prior to that point made it impossible to significantly raise my grade point average. I can vividly remember going to the department chair in my chosen major (my third major, but who was counting) and asking for a recommendation for graduate school. The professor looked at my grades and said to me with no sensitivity, "I can not give you a recommendation because you made a C in my class." I then asked an administrator at my college for a recommendation and his response was, "Do not embarrass this institution if you are admitted into graduate school." I knew that I was not very focused on academics during college, but the sad thing is that I didn't know any better. I didn't realize the significance of my undergraduate performance on my future.

Fortunately, the comments from others on my academic performance had no effect on my self-perception. I knew that I was intelligent despite my performance, even though others did not know it. I had to meet with the graduate admissions committee at my graduate school to explain my academic performance. It was probably one of the most embarrassing experiences of my life. I had a large committee of college professors looking at me as if I was stupid (based on my prior academic performance) and I had to explain why I did so poorly as an undergraduate. I distinctly remember looking into the eyes of one African American male representative on the committee. I felt a strong sense of compassion from him and disliked placing him in the position of probably having to defend my past in order to save my hide.

I knew that I could succeed in graduate school and I did. Despite my tumultuous beginning and at one time being considered an academic reject, I now have a Ph.D. They took a chance on me and it paid off. By all accounts, life has worked out wonderfully. I was able to overcome many obstacles including poverty, a single-parent home, ignorance of the collegiate experience, not being prepared academically for college, and many other life experiences. I was able to succeed because of faith, actions, support, and perseverance. Despite my background and abilities, a little faith (mixed with a lot of hard work) has taken me from agony to my destiny.

20 Simple Truths for Making Decisions That Matter to Young People
By Kim Crayton

What I Wish I Had Been Told

1. Seek Balance. Life is seldom black and white.
2. Don't ask a question unless you can handle the answer.
3. If it feels wrong, it is wrong. Don't wait around trying to figure it out, just go.
4. Spend time figuring out: who you are, what you value, and where your boundaries are.
5. Understand that life is not fair, but life can be good.
6. Understand that you are only responsible for you and that is enough.
7. Learn to be forgiving. You will make mistakes.
8. Do not seek outside yourself what you do not have to give to yourself.
9. Live in the moment.
10. Love is an action, not a feeling.
11. Be brave. Do what scares the heck out of you.

KIM CRAYTON

12. Being popular is different from being unconditionally loved.

13. Have fun.

14. Words have power, be careful how you use them.

15. It is never about the other person, it is always about you.

16. Suspend judgment. Things may not be what they seemed at first.

17. Learning is life long; use what you can and discard the rest.

18. Learn from others' mistakes.

19. Learn to ask yourself, "Do I want to be right or do I want to be happy?"

20. Remember, this too shall pass.

Heroes
By Kirk Nugent

We left Jamaica dead broke!
In high school I had two pairs of pants

"Immigrants are taking all our good jobs,"
Middle America hissed.
"Go back on your banana boat"
Was the phrase of choice Negroes used when they
  dissed.
So for the longest, dad was unemployed
Mom underemployed
And summertime in school
I was still rocking those two pairs of corduroy.
Found the American dream to be a hoax,
And for my clothing, the kids in school had mad jokes.
It was like Def Comedy Jam
When the class clown assembled his boys.
But I knew from Jamaica
That empty barrels made the most noise.
Here we had food stamp, name brand, welfare Negroes
Turning their nose up, as if they were rich snobs.
I ignored it!

By fifteen I was reading investment books
By Charles Schwab,
And just like you saw on *In Living Color*, I had three jobs.
While kids in my class were unwrapping gifts
From under the Christmas tree,
I was reading *How to Win Friends and Influence People*
By Dale Carnegie.

While cats blasted Eric B and Run DMC
I was listening to tapes of Earl Nightengale
Reinforcing, "Persistence is the key."
Doing paradigm shifts with my reality,
Fighting my insanity,
While simultaneously trying
To escape from what was obviously
A dysfunctional family.
Picked up a pen and found escape through my poetry.
Where the average sucker saw obstacles, I saw
   opportunity.
And by eighteen I'd decided that working forty hours
Building someone else's dream was not for me!

Took the road less traveled and found peace within,
While most of the thugs that I went to school with
Found lodging in the criminal system.
Telling me the White man made them victims
And how much America was their enemy,
But idiots always
Confuse bad management with destiny.
Girls that lived to put broke immigrants down
For the entire school year,
I now see them with three kids,
No baby father and a part time job as a cashier.
While immigrants that I know who slept five to a bed
Went on to become aeronautical engineers.
My goals are written precisely and clear,
Most are already accomplished, the rest are near.
And I can recall that it wasn't too long ago
When I stepped off
Air Jamaica with darn near zero.
So call *me* Bruce Wayne or Clark Kent,
Cause I'm my OWN hero!

I've Come To Claim My Destiny
By Kirk Nugent

Today I set before you a blessing and a curse,
Today I give you the powers to govern your own
  universe.
Because by our words we're justified, by our words
  we're condemned.
Behold the knowledge that I send and be careful what
  you speak,
The vibrations of your thoughts will elevate you above
  the highest peak
Or it will bring you come crashing to your knees!
Ever notice that women who complain that,
"All men are dogs" always seem to wake up with fleas?

It is that simple:
My thoughts control my destiny!
So go tell my enemies
They can no longer get the best of me
For today I'm here to claim my destiny!
I've come to claim my birthright,
What is rightfully mine,
What was given to me from the Divine.
Today I'm here to let my light shine.
So I'm rolling up my sleeves
And I'm gritting my teeth
And I dare Life to try and derail my dreams.

For I've been in these trenches for centuries,
Paid my dues, never made a fuss.

I've labored long and I've suffered much,
But today I'm lacing up my boots,
I've got my mouthpiece in.
Somebody put my music on I'm making my way to the
    ring.
Go tell that dirty Devil that Kirk Nugent said,
"Not today baby, not today!"
You just ain't breaking me today!
I don't care if you hit me with heartaches, headaches and
    bills that are unpaid!
You're just not defeating me today.

Today I refuse to be broken,
I will not be denied!
Ain't nobody turning me around
And the same ain't bringing me down.
So you can step aside with you snide remarks and your
    belittling words
Your lying lips no longer hurt.
I will no longer deny who I am, just to be accepted by
    you.
No more will I tolerate you in my space
With that constant frown
Bringing my spirits down.
When you approach me, take off thy shoes for you're
    standing on holy ground.

For today I'm shedding my limitations,
Erasing my boundaries,
Removing borders and expanding frontiers.
Fear and failure can no longer flourish here.
I am here to pay a price and walk away with my Destiny
And from this stage I will boldly state it,
I will not bow,

I will not buckle,
And I will not be intimidated!

I am swimming out to meet my ship before it docks,
Today I am walking away from the flock,
I am turning my back to the herd.
No more tears to weep, no more poor little me.
I am walking away from the sheep.
For I am a lion!
And I refuse to eat, to sleep, to sit with the sheep.
I am defiant!
Five foot ten, one hundred and fifty-five pound giant.
And I do not fit among little people
With their little people's problems, and their little people's
    fear.
Tell me nothing of their limitations, all I see is
    possibilities.
For I am Kirk Nugent, and Life simply cannot break me!

Today I will run and not be weary,
Walk and not faint,
Persistence and tenacity ain't got nothing on me
As a matter of fact I'm telling 2003 exactly what she's
    gonna do for me!
I am here to claim my destiny.
I will not be moved,
Like DNA I am "living proof".
That Life cannot battle against the sword of my spirit,
Not when everything in my life is relative.
Even my blood type is **B positive**!

Self-pity has long lost her allure,
I told you, *I Don't Write About Depression no more.*

I am far from fragile, did not get out of bed this morning
  to fail,
I'm the best pound for pound
And certainly did not get dressed just to be turned
  around.
The turbulence doesn't terrify me.
Tell the thunder be gone!
I might be at the end of my rope but I'm tying a knot .
And By God I'm holding on!
I'm in the eye of the storm with no life vest; ship
  wrecked!
But today I'm treading water, I'm kicking in doors.
I'm just not swallowing this salt water no more.
If Life thinks that spiritually it can break me
Then somebody done lied
Because today I will not be swept away with the tide.
Today I will swim with the sharks and not be eaten.
Did not spend nine months in the womb,
Just to come out to be beaten.
Ain't nobody turning me around!

So today I'm bubbling, I'm bursting,
I'm sowing, I'm reaping,
I'm paddling my own canoe this evening.
I've rekindled the fire in my eyes,
And God it feels good to be alive!
Somebody get me a pulpit I feel a need to testify.
For I ain't what I wanna be
Ain't what I'm gonna be,
But thank God, I ain't what I used to be.
I've been redeemed y'all.
New day, new destiny.
My eyes have been opened and I can no longer be
  deceived

Because back when I lacked knowledge, I used to
    believe.
Two years ago I used to believe my own alibi,
A year ago I used to believe that I was passion
personified
Six months ago I used to believe that Kirk Nugent could
    not be denied.
But thank God, I no longer believe,
I no longer believe that I can be denied
Because today I know, I CAN FLY!

The Pains of Education
By Lawana S. Gladney, Ph.D

The experience of working on my undergraduate degree was very challenging and presented a series of personal and academic struggles. Reflecting back on my arrival to campus as a freshman, I thought that the world was mine and studying did not belong in my world. Besides, what was studying anyway? I hadn't learned any study skills in high school. I was finally "grown" and could decide what classes I wanted to take—and whether or not I even went to class. I was a responsible young adult, so "responsible" that I was placed on academic probation after the second semester. With a GPA of 1.9, I was in such a predicament that there was nowhere to go but up or out.

After another semester, I managed to get my GPA up to 2.0, and by the second year, I transferred to a university out of state. Although my GPA was up to 2.1, the College of Education would not accept students with a GPA lower than a 2.5. Raising my GPA to a 2.5 seemed an insurmountable task when I considered the fact that I already had four D's on my transcript. However, this situation awakened my senses and forced me to realize that I was in college for one reason – *to graduate!*

After struggling for another year with a D, and at my lowest moment an F showing up on my transcript, I made a 180-degree turnaround. It was crystal clear - I had two years to get my act together. In the end, with a lot of hard work and the adoption of better study habits,

I managed to graduate with an overall GPA of 2.5, and a 3.1 in my final 60 undergraduate hours.

After all the challenges, you would have thought that I had enough of school. As life would have it, I married my college sweetheart and five years later, I was enrolled in school again. This time, it was as a graduate student. By this point, I had matured and I was determined to get the most out of my experience. And believe it or not, this time the university was *paying for my education* through an academic scholarship. I was offered the scholarship because the guidelines required a 3.0 GPA or better in your last 60 hours. Because I had a 3.1 GPA, I was a perfect fit for the program. Who would have thought that a little hard work and studying would pay such big dividends? Even I was surprised.

After two years, a summer and two babies later, I completed my Masters degree with a GPA of 3.6. Talk about an accomplishment! No one in my family had ventured to go that far with their education. During my last semester before graduation, one of the professors offered me the opportunity to apply for the doctorate program. A successful application would continue my scholarship. Although this was quite an honor, I had a dilemma. I was married with two small children and a third on the way. In addition, I was running a business and had started a mentoring program for teenage girls. Should I pursue another degree (for free) or should I stop here?

With the blessing of my spouse and the assistance of my support system, I decided that there was no way that I could turn down that kind of offer. And to think, these people really thought that I was smart! I had grown from the girl that was on academic probation to a woman accepted into the doctoral program.

The doctoral program was challenging. It wasn't that the coursework was so difficult, but the fact that a committee of six people was in charge of my destiny proved unsettling. I heard many stories of individuals who had completed all their course requirements, but never managed to complete the dissertation process because of their committees. Well, I determined that that wasn't going to happen to me. What I had to realize was that this committee was really in control of my future. I had to accept the fact that someone else, not me, would decide when I would graduate, and how I would graduate, or if I would even graduate at all.

The pivotal point in my school career occurred in the midst of writing my dissertation. I wrote it very well and followed the guidelines, or so I thought. The chair of my committee wanted the dissertation to be written in a format different than what I wrote. This would mean that I would have to re-write everything I had done, which also meant that I would have to be in school another semester. That was definitely not in my plan. Adding another semester was in direct conflict with my agenda. The fact that my education was free was not enough to carry me through at that time.

To say that I was totally discouraged and wanted to quit the program would be an understatement. Yes, that's what I decided to do. I didn't need the stress or the doctorate degree to prove who I was and what I could do. This situation offered insight and understanding why there are only a few people who actually finish their doctorate. Would I become one of those people?

Fortunately for me, one of my wise colleagues offered the advice, "Give them what they want just to get finished. When you get out, you can do what you want." After careful thought, I knew that I didn't really want to throw away all my hard work. After all, look what I had gone through to get this far. His words were the medicine that I needed to get me back on track. I humbled myself and rewrote my paper the way that the chair wanted. I finished a semester later than planned and successfully defended my dissertation with great pride.

When I look back on it all, I always had the option to quit. I could have made the decision to bow out, but I would be forced to say, "I am *almost* a doctor." Through all the ups, downs, challenges, sleepless nights, academic probation, failed tests, skipped classes, and 19 semesters of college, I can proudly say it was all worth it. The key is to not let anyone or anything steal your dreams. We all make choices with our lives, and whatever you choose to do, just make sure that you can be proud of your choices.

Not Again
By Lee Howard

"It's malignant."

I'll never forget those words. I had to hear them when my grandmother said them. I had to hear them when my grandfather said them. I even heard them when the veterinarian said them about my cat. In a matter of two years, I'd heard these words too many times. And then I heard it again from my dad. I remember saying to myself, "When does it stop?! I'm not even out of high school and I've lost my grandparents and I am about to lose my dad."

Mom and I tried everything. We kept him in the best spirits that we could. We encouraged him daily. We tried prayer, experimental medication, alternative medication, prayer, more prayer, and more prayer. Nothing was working. We were losing. Dad was dying.

I remember one day I was walking into a drug store to pick up a prescription for him. It was a pretty nice day outside. Birds were singing, people were smiling and laughing. But, I wasn't. I looked up at the sky as if I were speaking face to face with God and said, "He can't fight it anymore. He's tired. Give it to me instead." I'll never forget saying that. They say whatever doesn't kill you makes you stronger. They're right.

After nine months of fighting to live, Dad passed away. After a while, Mom and I started moving on with our lives. We started to have some happy days thrown into the mix of sad days. Things were looking up and we were ready to face the future with high hopes.

Then one day, I came down with a pretty bad cold. Usually, I would be rid of a cold in a few days, but I couldn't shake this one for some reason. After about two weeks of this, I decided to see a doctor. They ran a series of tests on me, trying to determine the cause of my unexplainable prolonged illness. The doctor found sufficient reason for me to see a specialist. Mom decided it would be best if she went with me for my next visit.

When the results came back from yet another series of tests, we had to hear those words again. The doctor dryly said, "It's malignant." I was overcome with emotion. I looked at Mom and saw tears rolling down her face. I was terrified, but I held in the fear for her sake. I told her I knew that I could beat it. I had to beat it. There was no do-over in this game. I knew this was going to be the biggest fight of my life--*for my life*.

The doctor referred me to a surgeon and I made an appointment for an operation shortly thereafter. After surgery, my body was a wreck. I had lost about 25 pounds in one week. The boy that used to be a healthy-looking athlete all of a sudden looked anorexic. Even my cheeks were sunken in due to the rapid weight loss. However, I felt much better mentally. I hadn't felt more full of life in weeks. I was rid of the cancer, so I thought.

Then, the surgeon came in to give me the news. The cancer had spread to my lymph nodes. Just when I thought the battle was over, I had to go see an oncologist. He explained to me that the best treatment for my situation would be chemotherapy for one year.

Physically and mentally, that year was the toughest year of my life. Chemotherapy can really mess you up, not only your body, but your mind, too.   My chemotherapy treatment was once a week, every week for the entire year. Every Thursday, I would go to the cancer center, sit in the chair, turn on Oprah, and let the nurse pump the poison into my blood. At first, it wasn't that bad. For a few weeks, I didn't even get sick. I remember thinking, "Heck, this is easy! Bring it on!! I can take this!" And then the nausea started.

Every Thursday after chemo, I would get sick. That's when it started playing with my mind. That's when I started to doubt. It got to the point that I would get sick before I even walked into the building for treatment. I couldn't even stand the smell of the place. One of the nurses told me that this was common with chemo patients. She told me that one of her patients was at home watching a story on the news about the cancer center. When her doctor appeared on screen, she automatically threw up! I could definitely relate.

Thank God I had my friends and family to lean on. I don't know if I would have made it if they weren't there for me. Whenever I thought I couldn't do another treatment, they were there to cheer me on and push me to the finish line. Whenever I needed help getting schoolwork finished, they were there to help me study. I was able to finish chemotherapy, beat cancer, graduate from high school, and start planning my future.

Some people don't see it this way, but I think I'm lucky and even blessed. I learned so much about life at such an early age. I learned to never give up on your hopes and most importantly to never give up on God. You see, I left out a part of my story. I mentioned earlier that I had asked God to give me the cancer and take it from my dad. What I didn't mention was that weeks later after that incident, when Dad was about to pass away, I stood on my bed, at yelled at God, "I hate You! I

HATE YOU!" I had given up on Him. Months later, I was asking for His help again. During the time of my illness, there wasn't a day that I didn't talk to Him. And since then, there hasn't been a day that I haven't thanked him for blessing me.

I could have surrendered and let the disease take me like it took my family members. Instead, I decided to fight. Through my struggle to stay alive, I learned that no matter what obstacles you face in life, you must never surrender, never give up, and never stop believing. You never know what you can accomplish until you try.

Happiness Is a Pair of Shorts!
By Manuel Diotte

Life! What a precious gift from God. What a blessing to be alive in a wonderful, vibrant world of unlimited possibilities. Then, adversity strikes, and this "gift" feels more like a curse. "Why? Why me?" we ask. Yet we never get an answer, or do we? After contracting Hodgkin's disease at age seven and being given six months to live, I triumphed over the odds. Call it luck, hope, faith or courage, there are thousands of survivors! Winners like us know the answer - "Why not us? We can handle it!" I'm not dying of cancer. I'm living with cancer. God doesn't make junk, regardless of what comes our way, and I don't have to be afraid anymore.

In my sophomore year of high school, the class was scheduled to run the mile. I will always remember that day because due to the swelling and scars from surgery on my leg, for two solid years I had not worn shorts. I was afraid of the teasing. So, for two years I lived in fear. Yet that day, it didn't matter. I was ready - shorts, heart and mind. I no sooner got to the starting line before I heard the loud whispers. "Gross!" "How fat!" "How ugly!" I blocked it out. Then the coach yelled, "Ready. Set. Go!" I jetted out of there like an airplane, faster than anyone for the first 20 feet. I didn't know much about pacing then, but it was okay because I was determined to finish first. As we came around the first of four laps, there were students all over the track. By the end of the second lap, many of the students had already quit. They had given up and were on the ground gasping for air. As I started the third lap, only a few of my classmates were left on the track, and I began limping. By the time I hit the fourth lap, I was alone. Then it hit me. I realized that nobody had given up. Instead, everyone had already finished. As I ran that last lap, I cried. I realized that every boy and girl in my class had beaten me, and 12 minutes, 42 seconds after starting, I crossed the finish line. I fell to the ground and shed oceans of tears. I was so embarrassed.

Suddenly, my coach ran up to me and picked me up, yelling, "You did it. Manuel! Manuel, you finished, son. You finished!" He looked me straight in the eye waving a piece of paper in his hand. It was my goal for the day, which I had forgotten. I had given it to him before class. He read it aloud to everyone. It simply said, "I Manuel Diotte, will finish the mile run tomorrow, come what may. No pain or frustration will stop me. For I am more than capable of finishing, and with God as my strength, I will finish." Signed, Manuel Diotte - with a little smiling face inside the D, as I always sign my name. My heart lifted. My tears went away, and I had a smile on my face as if I had eaten a banana sideways. My classmates applauded and gave me my first standing ovation. It was then I realized winning isn't always finishing first. Sometimes winning is just finishing.

MARCEL BRUNEL

See the Big Picture
By Marcel Brunel

A colleague once shared with me that a principle of life is a fundamental truth. It is true in any country, city, and or community. The principle my father taught me was *that for every short-term behavior there is a long-term consequence.* That principle is true in Korea, France, Nashville, Cuba, anywhere. Even in Grove City, Ohio.

When I was a young boy back in the 1970's, I was the third of five children. I spent most of my childhood in Grove City, Ohio. I had a face full of freckles and a smile from ear to ear. My father is a very smart man who worked hard to protect and provide for his family. In second grade my father introduced me into what my older brother and sister had known about for some time, it was called a paper route. The *Columbus Citizen Journal* was delivered mostly by bike at about 4:30 A.M. every day except Sunday. If there was a blizzard then you delivered the paper on sled. If the rain was pouring, then you would hide under the barbershop awning where you picked up your newspapers and bagged them tight to be ready for the long and wet morning ahead.

I was seven years old with my older brother and sister learning something no book in the world could ever explain, instruct, or pontificate about. My father was teaching each of his children the idea of "with." He was always with us. My father did nothing *for* us or *to* us. It was all *with* us. None of my friends understood why my father would get us up every morning at 4:30

A.M. and help us deliver our newspapers. When we were done, he made hot chocolate for us while we all roasted our toes and hands over the heat vents in the floor. There were many mornings when the urge to *give up* instead of *get up* had a better ring to it. Many times, my father shared with us the need to keep going and how important it was for us to see past what we were feeling at that moment.

There were many mornings while we were out delivering the newspaper that I really didn't want to do my part. I had grown tired of having to do the same thing over and over again, day after day. As much as I complained, I never remember my father allowing me to sit out one day. He did not confuse the concept of "performance" versus "convenience." I wanted my life to be convenient, yet make the money of a top performer along the way. He knew that this wouldn't cut it in the "real world," so he never allowed us to quit. That lifestyle might have worked on television, but not in Grove City, Ohio. He explained to us again and again that what we were doing as young children would set the stage for what we would do once we were adults, out in the world on our own.

I delivered the newspaper from second through eighth grade. My younger brother and sister also became part of the process and my father remained there every step of the way. My father's daily doses of wisdom were more like spoonfuls of common sense. He taught his children how to show up on time, complete what you start, do what you say you are going to do, and say "please" and "thank you." All common sense yet, seldom, common practice. All of these "short-term behaviors" my father knew would have long-term consequences, as we got older. He made it hard on us from the beginning of our lives so it would be easier as we grew older.

Being a person of principle is a constant pursuit. Man did not create life's many principles, he discovered them. Edison did not create electricity, he discovered it. I am thankful now that at a young age, my father helped me discover life's principles and learn how they work.

My story is one that includes a man who taught me at a young age how to work. Through my work I learned about people, money, and personal growth. We all know it is easier to change your mind than it is to change your plan. Anybody can be critical, anyone can quit, anybody can "wing it" and not have a plan.

Ask someone you respect, value, and trust to help you co-create a plan for your faith, your family, and your future. Constantly ask yourself this question, "How does one see?" These are the four most powerful words put together by man. How one sees his or her life is usually how one treats his or her life. How one sees their friends is most often the way one treats their friends. In my case, my father taught me to see life in the big picture rather than as a set of isolated events. He taught me that what I do now directly affects what I will have in the future.

All five of my parents' children went to college, graduated, and paid for our own awesome educations. My father and mother have been married now for 40 years and have seven grandchildren. I have been married to my wife of eight years and two children and another on the way. I look forward to being "with" each of my children and instilling in them that same eternal and infinitely valuable principle: *Every short-term behavior has a long-term consequence.*

Money, Love & 'Da Dream Job
By Sanyika Calloway Boyce

My journey on the path to financial fitness began with much anxiety and almost by accident. Upon graduation from college, I had all the hopes of a wonderful life ahead. With a degree in my hand, a dream job on my mind, and a pile of debt in my pocket — I started out in the world. However, my hopes of success quickly came to a halt as I discovered I was not ready for the real world.

I had no idea how the debt in my pocket would alter my life in such a dramatic way. I came from a school of thought that said, "You can't squeeze blood from a turnip." Basically speaking, if you don't have it, they (the creditors) can't get it. I had no idea that they indeed had a way of getting it (the money you owe), or at the least the ability to make life unbearable in the process.

I wasn't really trying to dodge those creditors to whom I owed a collective $15,000. I was simply putting them off for a minute. The idea was to land my dream job, make good money, pay all the old creditors (I owed money on ten credit cards), and maybe start fresh by getting a few new creditors. Thus, proving that I was a good and responsible person and not the deadbeat I was made out to be.

As I stepped onto the path of life after college ready to make my dreams of career, money, and love a reality, I learned the truth; how you handle money matters. It plays a big part in how others perceive you, whom and how you love, and the career you choose or are forced to choose.

SANYIKA CALLOWAY BOYCE

This realization came after learning that I was not going to get my dream job. Not because I wasn't qualified, in fact, they loved me and wished they could make an exception to hire me. However, because I had made several bad decisions regarding my credit, it was impossible for me to get a job that came with an expense account and a credit card. I was devastated. No one warned me. I had no idea how far bad credit could reach. Unfortunately, I was about to find out.

As though the career blow wasn't enough to keep me on the straight and narrow, I continued to make unwise financial decisions, like:

- Co-signing for a friend's car loan.
- Trying to pay a "Credit Doctor" to wipe my credit report clean.
- Getting taken by a consolidation scam.

Finally, I decided that the process of getting out of debt and becoming financially fit was up to me.

On the journey to new found financial freedom, I thought I was the only one in the world to mess things up so bad. But, as I walked the rough, sometimes confusing, and always interesting path of managing money, finding love, and landing the dream job, I came across many weary travelers. I met other good people who'd made bad decisions.

I found out very quickly that there was no book, tape, pill, or potion. But, it was a combination of information and techniques that worked.

Although it took me more than four years of struggle and sacrifice to repay my debt, I would not change the experience. It taught me a few things that I'm happy to share:

- Credit isn't the same as cash. Use both wisely.
- Love's got a whole lot to do with it when the rent's due.
- We must each hold ourselves accountable- the creditors will!
- There is no victory without struggle and sacrifice.
- A budget is telling your money where to go, rather than wondering where it went.
- Asking for help is the best way to get it.

And...In the profound but simple words of Henry Ford, "Whether you think you can or think you can't you're always right"

Financial fitness can be yours! Go out and claim it!

Soul Tests
By Sean Stephenson

When I was born I brought with me into this world a rare bone condition called, Osteogenesis Imperfecta. This condition causes the bones to be extremely fragile and stunted in growth. The shortest trip I have ever taken in life, through the birth canal, was so physically traumatic that my frail bones snapped like tiny twigs being jammed through the eye of a needle.

The doctors informed my frightened parents that I wouldn't make it through the first night of my life. Fortunately, I had other plans. I was immediately transferred in an ambulance from Memorial Hospital to Children's Hospital in Chicago. My father and grandfather rode along next to me on that half-hour ride into the big city. As they neared the hospital the ambulance drove right past DePaul University. Like ships passing in the night, it was at that moment that my future encountered my present, offering a wink and a whisper of hope. My dad and grandpa had no clue if I would live to see my first birthday, let alone manage to attend college eighteen years later across the street from the very hospital where my life was in jeopardy.

As the years passed, I watched as my classmates grew taller, but I never did. God kept my soul in a package that could never exceed three feet tall. Living in a tiny body has been difficult but it isn't my greatest challenge. While my friends were outside running and screaming for joy I was often inside screaming in pain. By the time I turned 18, I had experienced over 200 bone fractures. Something as simple as sneezing could snap a collarbone or a few ribs, leaving me to several weeks of healing.

The one thing that has never been broken has been my spirit. As a professional speaker I travel the country speaking to students, just like you, about the importance of "loving life." One time while on stage, a curious teenager dressed in big baggy jeans and an oversized T-shirt asked nervously, "Would you trade your physical condition if you could?" As I sat up on stage holding my microphone and slowly scanning the audience with my eyes, a smile grew on my face like a blossoming flower. I took a breath and then declared to the universe, "No my friend, I wouldn't trade it for the world. Although it may appear that my challenges are overwhelming, the gifts are plenty. Who I am, what I know, and what I can do is a collection of beauty. Trading my challenges would mean I would have to trade my knowledge, experience, and strength and that I wouldn't, nor ever want to do." I went on to tell the young man and the rest of his high school peers in the audience that I wasn't always comfortable with my physical condition.

Living through high school is tough. I know it was for me. Most teenagers are frustrated with their search for their own identities. The reality is they will never find it. This is because you have to create your identity, it's never found. I began creating my identity at the age of only seven.

It was Halloween morning and I was playing around in my living room when all of a sudden I snagged my Halloween costume on the corner of the door. The snag snapped my right femur from the impact. While holding my right leg in excruciating pain I cried out, "Why me God? What did I ever do to deserve this? I am just a little boy." In order to calm me down my mother gently posed a very powerful question. "Sean, is this physical condition going to be a gift or a burden in your life?"

As I lay on the floor clenching my fists in agony, a feeling of clarity surrounded the truth of my condition. I was experiencing something everyone alive experiences...pain! We all have pain, how we deal with our pain makes all the difference. I realized I could empathize with people in pain and that I had something in common with everyone. I saw my challenge as a gift. My soul was being tested in that moment, and it would be tested everyday forward. My condition administers "pop quizzes" quite frequently.

All of our physical and emotional challenges are just tests for our souls. How well we do is determined by how much we want to grow and learn from them. Some people choose never to show up to their tests, and because of this, they are constantly failing. The good news is we can study with partners and in groups for these tests. I know this because I have tutored thousands of individuals, often without even saying a word. I realized the power in soul tutoring when I rescued a complete stranger from failing the gift of life.

Boston Bill is the name that I'll always remember him by. My family and I were delayed from flying out of Boston one night while on vacation. It was late and there were no other flights leaving for Chicago that evening. So we called a hotel nearby and reserved a room. On the shuttle ride from the airport to our hotel I shared smiles and laughter with our bus driver Bill. When we arrived I said goodbye to Bill and we went our separate ways. I chalked our friendly conversation up to pleasant customer service, not knowing the magnitude of our interaction.

While eating a late dinner with my family in the hotel restaurant Bill approached our table. "Do you mind if I give Sean a hug?" he asked my parents. Bill then shared with my family his life tragedies. His wife died, his kids wouldn't speak with him, and he had been in therapy. He continued by saying that he had been contemplating suicide for quite sometime. After meeting me and seeing how I handled my challenges with love and laughter he found a renewed sense of purpose for his life. He then said with tears rolling down his cheeks, that observing only a few minutes of my attitude was more life altering than years of therapy. Bill no longer wanted to end his life because he saw the beauty in his soul tests.

You may be where Bill was. Frustrated, angry, and/or feeling hopeless. There isn't a single person on the planet that hasn't thought of throwing in the towel. Giving up may seem like the best option at times but it always turns out to be the worst. You never know what wonderful gifts your challenges can be unless you stick around to finish your tests.

If you take anything from my story, take this: You and I will endure many bumps, bruises, and even breaks along the way. But our souls remain perfectly intact. Your soul has an unlimited amount of potential. You were born for a positive reason and your time here on earth is precious. The tests may be hard and at times not seem fair but the lessons you learn will cause you to graduate life with HIGH HONORS.

Still Standing!
By Sean Watkins

It seems hard now, but trust me, you can make it.
Just stand.

My parents are divorced and have been for a number of years. My dad is a very nice man, but he's also an alcoholic. He was never around much. He came around on birthdays and Christmas time. When I was in the 5th grade, my mom's personal problems forced me to live with him until I came to college. My dad could drive from Canada to Texas and not say a word the entire trip. That was really hard to deal with growing up. There are so many things that you want to talk about with your parents, but my dad would never say anything. I'd become so accustomed to us not talking, I began to deal with problems on my own. It forced me to grow up a head of time.

I remember a time when my dad was driving me back from Karate practice. He had arrived early and saw me. To my surprise, we actually talked during the trip home. I talked more with my dad in those fifteen minutes than all other times put together. He told me of how he was in martial arts, but as he was telling his story, he missed the exit for our house. "Damn," he said, and not another word after that. It was as though he blamed our talking for his lapse in concentration. Sadly enough, that comment concluded what was the only real conversation we ever had.

You always see the commercials, "Talk to your kids. You can talk to your parents." It never happened. I would ask my mom, "Why doesn't he talk to me?" She would simply say, "That's just the way he is." Have you ever wished you could pick your parents? Anyhow, I'm standing.

Let me introduce you to my mother. She, on the other hand, is one of the sweetest people you could ever meet. She's intellectual, brown-skinned, 5'4"(though she acts like a giant) and hails from a little town called Crockett, Texas. She graduated at the top of her class from Yates High School in Houston, Texas as well as from Texas Southern University. She taught elementary school for 25 years. My mom trusts everyone, and I mean everyone. She forgives at the blink of eye, and gives unconditionally. But my mom has a problem.

My dad had an affair, which lead to my parent's divorce. This was her second failed marriage, as her first husband committed suicide. She blamed herself, figuring that there must have been something wrong with her to have two marriages that didn't work. Unable to cope with the pressure, my mother turned to crack cocaine, hoping to ease her woes. She started when I was six years old. I am now twenty.

For fourteen years, my mom was a drug addict. She was in and out of hospitals, only to go back to drugs each time. You could tell that she wanted to do better, but her addiction was too strong for her. She never received any support from the family when she got a divorce, especially when her addiction surfaced. Rehabilitation emphasizes the importance of family support, but there was none. Thus, she would continually return to the life she desperately sought to get away from.

I can remember one time when my mother had been sober for six months, but the neighborhood she lived in made drugs all too accessible. In the blink of an eye, she relapsed. At one point, I saw my mother try to jump from a three-story apartment to get a hit because her craving was so strong that it made her hallucinate. Her boyfriend had to hold her down to prevent her from jumping. As powerful as my mother was mentally and spiritually, her addiction was just as powerful, perhaps more.

When I got to the 12th grade, I told my mother she couldn't come to my graduation. I was graduating at the top of my class. I was in the top 1% of my class, Male Valedictorian, Most Outstanding Male Student, and I didn't want my mom to come to my graduation for fear that she would show up under the influence of drugs. It would kill me. I told her, "I'm graduating next Spring, and if you don't get yourself together, I'd rather you didn't come see me graduate."

I had issues of my own that I had to deal with. I had a lack of self-confidence. I didn't know what to do with my life or even if college was for me. I applied to the University of Texas for the sole purpose of obtaining scholarships—I hadn't filled out any other applications. Reverend Lawson, the pastor of my church and my personal mentor that knew my entire story. He told me, "You cannot come this far to stop. You have so many storms, but stand strong and stand through them. Just stand." And you know what? He was right! I realized that God had carried me too far through the storm to leave me. I knew He was with me, and with Him, I could do anything.

Just as I began to feel a lot better about my future, I was once again broken down when I received a letter from UT stating that I waited too late to apply, and that I wouldn't be allowed admission. I was *really* down this time. I felt like a gush of wind was knocked out of my chest. But then I remembered that I am here for a reason. I remembered that I can look *at* my circumstances, or I can look *through* my circumstances. I can stand and persevere. I said to myself, "Hey, I'll apply to other schools. I didn't even want to go there. I'll start applying for scholarships, too."

I was only two months away from graduation. Every scholarship I applied for, I received. I got accepted to Emory University in Atlanta, Sam Houston State University, Texas Southern University, St. Louis University, the list goes on. I spoke at the induction ceremony for the Chancellor of Texas A&M University. He said, "Sean, when you graduate, if you want to come to A&M, give me a call. I'll take care of the rest." I said to myself, "Alright, God, I see you working." Then UT sent me a letter one day, and said they just received my transcript.

"Top one percent? We are so sorry for the mix up," the letter read. "WELCOME TO THE UNIVERSITY OF TEXAS!"

All I did was continue to stand.

My mother came to my graduation a proud, sober parent. My dad came drunk. My mom and I began the long and tedious process of trying to rebuild our relationship and regain the time that was lost. The only problem was that, although I was eighteen, she had the mindset that I was still six years old. That was the last time that we had a real relationship. We argued constantly. It was something that we both were unprepared for. We still had many problems to resolve. On the other side, my dad still drank like a fish. Somehow, I continued to stand.

The day my sophomore year of college started, my mother called my house using a voice I thought I would never hear again. It was the voice that raised me for most of my life, and the voice that I had grown to hate. She turned back to drugs. I was devastated. Nothing mattered to me. I took on a careless attitude that transcended into other areas of my life. Though previously I worked exceptionally hard at them, I let my academics, organizations, and all responsibilities slide. I didn't care about the consequences.

I was on the verge of losing all of my scholarships. Again, I leaned on one of my mentors to share my troubles. He cried. He told me, some students had contemplated suicide with far less on their plates. He told me, "Sean, you are unbelievably strong. Don't give up now, just stand firm, you'll make it." So I did. I stood.

With each passing day, my mother's sobriety level increases. She plans to see me graduate from college with two years sobriety, God willing. My dad drinks nowhere near as much anymore. Why? Only God knows. As for me, I'm standing. I know God wouldn't carry me this far to drop me. He wants me to persevere, and I want to. All I can do is give it my all, then stand.

Miracle or Mess, Insist on Being Blessed
By Shorty King

When I was in the 8th grade, my Social Studies teacher called me "stupid," made me stand in the back of the room for about 20 minutes, then sent me to the principal's office for detention. Three miraculous things happened for me as a result of this incident.

The teacher must have been having a bad day, because I wasn't the only person that she sent to the office that day. I was fortunate to have a good reputation, so the principal listened to my side of the story. He decided not to give me detention, or send a letter home. Instead, he encouraged me to respect the fact that teachers are human and that they sometimes say things they don't mean. He sent me on to my next class. Yes—Miracle #1.

Parents *always* want to know about your day, even when they don't ask. Sometimes they don't ask because they don't want to seem nosey, or don't want you to feel like they don't trust you. So I decided to tell my mother about my day. Actually, I was still feeling a little hurt about being called "stupid" and I really wanted to hear my mother tell me that I was smart. Parents forget to do that sometimes, and my mother was no exception.

Well, my mother couldn't believe what had happened to me, and said she'd call and discuss the incident with my school. My mother had *never* previously taken my side against a teacher. As it turned out, this was the only time she did. Trust me, this qualified as Miracle #2. She made clear her belief that teachers had a tough enough job because she knew that kids were not all angels, sometimes more like demons. Though she did actually take the time to investigate matters this time, my mother was certain to instill some lessons in the process. She reminded me of a few things:

- No one has the right to call you stupid.
- Just because someone calls you a name doesn't mean you are what they call you.
- Teachers are human.
- If you have a good reputation, people will listen to you.
- If you do what you're supposed to do, even adults will listen to you.
- Positive things can come from negative experiences.

As it turned out, I had another 8th grade teacher whose positive action opened the way for far more miraculous things to happen in my life. Her name was Georgina Land. Ms. Land was my science teacher, and the person who recommended me for the ABC Scholarship Program. ABC (A Better Chance) awards academic financial assistance so that low-income families can send their kids to private high schools. Enter Miracle #3. I earned a three-year trip to Cranwell School, an all-boys Jesuit prep school in Lenox, Massachusetts.

You might think that I was an honor roll student, a sports star, nerd, teacher's pet or related to someone with clout. How about "none of the above?" Oh, I admit I was pretty popular because I had a good sense of humor (that's my positive way of saying I was one of the class clowns), yet I doubt that my showmanship is what inspired Ms. Land to see how much potential I had. For some reason, she believed that I was one of the kids who could succeed if given a new set of options. Ms. Land trusted her instincts to believe in me, hoping that a change in scenery would inspire me to do more with my life.

During my sophomore year in high school, I started writing poetry to combat homesickness. To my surprise, I discovered that I had a gift for expressing myself through my writing. It helped me get my point across in a creative and calm way, rather than the destructive measures that could have landed me on the wrong side of trouble. I began to enjoy my secret talent for connecting thoughts to paper. It was as if I was able to see a collection of my thoughts on paper for the first time. I never would have thought I'd be writing poetry about my inner feelings. After all I grew up thinking that "feelings" were for girls. Yet, through this art form, I was introduced to a person that I thought I knew before, but really didn't—myself. As I read and reread my poems, I became increasingly in tune with who I was on the inside, though at the time, I wasn't quite ready to share it with people.

As I got to know myself better, I became more excited about being successful. I began to understand that there was something special that God had given me. That special "something" made me unique from every other person in my world, and it made me feel important. I started to see the great student that Ms. Land saw. I began to trust my instincts that pushed me to keep doing my best and to frequently share my gift. Eventually, people started asking me to write poems for them, and telling me that my poetry captured exactly how they felt.   During my senior year, my English teacher wrote on one of my papers, "Your essays are a joy to read." As I continued to lose myself in my poetry, the power of the written word became so clear to me that I began to see it as my ticket to future success.

I joined the National Speakers Association in 1995 to concentrate on learning how to market my speaking business, using my poetry. I joined Toastmasters that same year to combine my natural abilities with the skills of a polished speaker.   In 1996, I competed for the Toastmasters World Championship of Public Speaking and finished as one of the Top 9 speakers in the world!

Miraculous? Maybe. There's a saying that reminds us not to believe in miracles, but to insist on them. I also submit that sometimes we have to just wait on the miracle, look back, and laugh at what we went through in order to have it unfold. As I think back to my 8th grade miracles I'm reminded that:

- I obviously was not stupid. Actually, I was "a miracle in motion."
- Though my teacher put me in a painful situation, it was the platform for my miracle.
- As I got to know myself better it became easier to gain other people's respect.
- As I became a more positive person, people acted more positively toward me.
- As I nurtured my gift, I improved my performance in school and found great success in life.

My "mess" introduced me to my miracles. My miracles introduced me to my future love–the power of words. Because of this, I now look for the positive things in life, especially during negative situations. I stand a believer that tough times can't kill me, they can only make me stronger. I insist on being blessed!

A Dream Deferred
By Tiffany Pertillar

Being a senior in high school is supposed to be a memorable time. You're an upperclassman who gets to start planning for college. It's the last EVERYTHING! It's the last big football game and the last homecoming. It's growing up and having that last year of fun with people who have been your friends for twelve years. It's the senior prom with that special date. To top it all off, you have graduation as a reward for all of your years of hard work. Graduation day—you're finally an "adult" and the rest of your life can begin. Right after graduation you and your friends get in the car and head straight to the beach for Senior Week. Being a senior is supposed to be one of the greatest times of your life, however, that was not my experience at all.

My experience was memorable but for different reasons. Instead of planning for college, I was planning for a baby. I didn't even go to the last football game, although it was my final outing as a senior cheerleader. Hanging out with my friends became a thing of the past. I pushed everything and everyone that I loved away from me. Senior prom? That was a joke. Nobody wanted to take a girl that was as big as a house to the prom. Instead of going off to the beach for Senior Week, I sat in my house with my mom and dad. I didn't have a chance to experience everything that a normal seventeen-year-old kid gets to experience, and it was nobody's fault but my own.

My teenage years were tumultuous to say the least. I was raised in a Christian home, and I accepted Christ into my life when I was twelve. After I accepted Christ, I was "on fire for God" for a little while. I was all about God and doing His will, but when I entered high school, things just went down hill. I became a cheerleader, and hung out with the "popular crowd". I started down a long and self-destructive road. I began dating guy after guy and somewhere along the way I lost sight of myself and what was really important to me.

It all came crashing down around me when I met a guy named Tony. Tony was amazing. He was 6'5, dark, handsome, and not to mention the greatest sweet talker I had ever met! Tony and I started to date and I completely thought that I wanted to be with him forever. I was sixteen. What did I know?

Things were going great, and then Tony started asking me to have sex with him. For a while I was adamant about saying no, but then I let my guard down. After months of asking, I finally gave in. The first time that I had sex with Tony was my first and my last sexual experience. I got pregnant on October 2, 1998, just after my seventeenth birthday. I was in the first semester of my senior year of high school.

Let me remind you again, I was raised in a strict Christian home. To make matters worse, my father used to be a pastor. Getting pregnant just wasn't an option, not for someone who wasn't even supposed to be having sex. I felt the pressure of having gone against everything that I believed in, as well as the public embarrassment that I brought to my entire family.

I couldn't believe that I got pregnant. I thought, "How could I, of all people be pregnant?" All of my friends were having sex, but I was the one who got "caught" on her first time. It didn't seem fair. I was mad at myself, mad at Tony, and even had the audacity to be mad at God. I failed to realize that all the while, it was my fault! My situation was a direct result of a decision that I'd made. But the wonderful God that I serve had a plan all along. He was using my mistake to change my life. He wanted me to start living for Him, but in order for that to happen I had to realize that I *needed* Him. I had to hit rock bottom before I could fully understand the power of God.

So, I had some decisions to make. I am ashamed to even admit this, but my first thought was that I was going to have an abortion and my parents were never going to find out. I didn't want that baby, and it wasn't going to ruin my life. Pretty selfish of me, huh? When I finally came to my senses, I realized that I had already made an error by having sex in the first place. I couldn't kill my unborn child to run away from my "problem". After I thought about it, the abortion was out of the question.

When I told Tony, he also suggested that I have an abortion. He acted as if I had planned to get pregnant, like it was in my plans to have a child in high school. I gave him a choice, he could either stay and we could do this together, or he could leave and I would do it by myself. Either way, my child was going to be born. Tony was terrified at the notion of becoming a teenaged father. You can guess what he opted to do.

When Tony decided to leave, it hit me that I would have to raise this baby on my own. However, I didn't even have a high school diploma yet. I had no education, no job and I had absolutely no money. All I knew was that I loved this child with all of my heart and

I only wanted to the best for him. I knew that I couldn't be a capable provider. He deserved much more than I could ever give him. I thought, prayed, cried, and prayed some more. Finally, I decided to place my son up for adoption. It was the hardest decision I had ever made, but it was clearly the best thing I could have done for him.

I graduated from high school, waddling across the stage to accept my diploma. One month later, I had a beautiful baby boy. I spent three short days with my son while we were in the hospital. They were the three best days of my life. He is an amazing little boy and I never knew that I could love someone so much. He is a blessing, not only to my family and me, but also to the wonderful family that adopted him.

It wasn't in God's plan for my life to be a mother at the age of seventeen. My son was an accident but he surely wasn't a mistake. God doesn't make mistakes. My son's life has changed my life. I am stronger now. I have a clear direction and an undeniable plan for my future. I had no clue as to who I was or what I was doing, but God did. He knew that He was going to use my mistakes for His Glory. I wouldn't have had go through so much hurt and pain if I had just trusted in the Lord from the very beginning—but I was stubborn and living the way that I wanted to live. Now I live for God and He is leading me towards marvelous places. I'm not perfect, and I still have a long way to go on this journey, but instead of traveling it alone, I'm leaning on God's everlasting arms. I couldn't do it any other way.

I am now a senior in college, and in May of 2003 I am going to graduate with a BS in Human Services. After graduation, I plan on attending law school. My ultimate goal is to become a lawyer for children who need to be adopted or placed in foster homes, and then eventually I want to open up a house for pregnant teenage girls. I know what it's like. I know how hard it is. But I also know that there is light at the end of the tunnel. Through God, all things are possible. If I can get through it, anybody can.

Light as a Pen, Heavy as a Spade
A Grandmother's Wit
By Tony Magee, MS, MBA

TONY MAGEE

It felt like the inside of an oven – outside on that hot summer day in 1978. My team was up by two touchdowns and Jimmy passed me the pig's skin. I ran as fast as I could – darting left, then faking right as I headed for the end zone. I was flawless – just like Tony Dorsett flying in the wind making another spectacular touchdown. Suddenly the air was filled with the sound of TONNNNNNY!!! I froze right in my tracks. I knew that sound and so I hollered back, "Yes Ma'am Mama!" She said, "Come home right this minute, I have some work for you to do." All my friends were upset mumbling, "Man Tony, we're almost finished with our game. Why does your grandmother always call you when we're having fun? Do you really have to go?" I said to them, "Yeah man, but if I don't go, she might whip me with her Mississippi strap. Look, it's embarrassing to get your behind whipped by a woman who's four-foot-nine when you're five-two. Man, I gotta go - I'll see y'all later."

I knew that if I did not respond with a quickness, Mama's threat would result in that strap across my behind. And believe me, I didn't want any part of it 'cause my grandmother knew how to whip.

When I got to the house, we headed for the backyard. Mama asked me to dig a hole for her new rose bush. That day, it was hotter than any July, all of Africa, two Indias and a Victorville. Mama said to me,

"Baby, I want you to take that there spade (a shovel) and dig Mama a hole for this here rose bush." Using her hands to emphasize the dimensions, she said, "Dig Mama a hole this big-of-round and this here deep." She instructed me to dig the hole near an old brick-walled fence away from the rest of her garden, where Mama like to plant her turnip, collard and mustard greens.

My face dripping with dirty- salty sweat, I took the spade and began digging the hole. Mama went inside the house to fix us some lemonade and said she would be back to check on me. As the sweat drenched my clothes and the inside of my mouth felt like I had just eaten a lemon - my mind drifted. I thought I smelled — Mama's good ol' southern fried chicken and hot water cornbread. Then I thought, "I'd give anything right now for a plate, but instead I have to dig this stupid hole." The time passed so slowly that with each beat of my heart, it seemed like an eternity.

Thirty minutes went by, then an hour, then an hour and fifteen minutes. I had not even gone two inches passed the top surface of the soil. Frustrated and thirsty I started getting mad at the dirt. I even kicked it a few times. I couldn't believe I was missing football to dig a hole in the ground. Finally, Mama returned to the backyard with a pitcher of ice-cold lemonade and two large jelly-jar glasses. She said, "You ain't finished diggin' my hole yet, Baby? What's taking you so long?" I told her "Mama this dirt is harder than steel."

Mama told me to take a break and have a glass of lemonade with her. I was happy because it was burnin' hot and Mama made that good kind of lemonade. It would be so good and sugar-sweet that you'd have to take your shoes off so you could wiggle your toes – it was that Mississippi stuff. I gulped down my first two glasses in less than a minute. After wiping my face and mouth with my dirty shirt, I told Mama "sorry I couldn't dig the hole for you. I tried Mama. I even have blisters on my hands to prove it."

Her voice was filled with compassion as she told me the reason I could not dig a hole in that particular area was because there was a block of excess cement just beneath the surface of the dirt - from that old brick fence. She said, "Baby, on the surface, the ground by that there fence looks the same as the rest of the yard. But ain't it funny how folk always say *'what you don't know won't hurt you?'* I want you to know *what you don't know can kill you.* You didn't know about that hidden chunk of concrete - now did you? Now tell me again - how does those blisters on your hands feel?"

Mama knew all along what she was doing. I was upset, but knowing Mama, she had a reason for it all. She was teaching me about life and education. She would sometimes discourage me from wanting to play so much with my little knuckle-headed friends. She said, "Children nowadays play entirely too much and think they know everything. What they need to know is the value of hard work, and spend more time preparing for their future. They need that down home kind of discipline. It takes a village to raise a little child, but if that village is crazy, then they will raise some very crazy kids. You are my grandchild and I want you to go to college some day and become more of yourself. I want you to have the best chance to live your best life. It's of great importance to me. You see, Mama didn't have all the great opportunities that you young folk take for granted today."

As a working farm girl from Clarksdale, Mississippi, my grandmother was only able to finish the ninth grade. Not because she wasn't bright – in fact, she was one of the smartest pupils in all of her classes. Mama and her eleven brothers and sisters all had to lend their hands to labor on Big Daddy's farm. She was wise to emphasize the value of education in my life.

In retrospect, this event has become the most important defining moment of my life. I often ask myself where would I have been without my grandmother's wisdom and her belief in me becoming a major success?

Surviving the poverty and violence within concrete-block walls of Watts Nickerson Gardens Housing Projects, earning a BS in Industrial Engineering, becoming the first African-American to receive a Master's degree in Material Science and Engineering from Lehigh University, an MBA from Pepperdine, completing Executive MBA studies at Oxford University in England and enjoying a quality life turned out to be the easiest things I'd ever accomplished. The hardest thing was believing that I could do it. My grandmother knew it and surely believed it. That's why we must always thank God for those who believe in us when we sometimes don't believe in ourselves.

As Mama would put it, *"Baby, with a good education, your life's work will be as light as a pen. Without it, your life's work will be as heavy as that spade."*

The Champion
By Tony Powell

To this very day it is hard for me to understand why she did the things that she did. To this day, I find it hard understand why I was the one who was most often on the receiving end of her attacks. A mother is someone who loves, nourishes, and builds character in her children. That is how I always felt it should be. Unfortunately, in my home, it was different.

It is difficult for me to recall my childhood as a good experience. The physical and mental abuse I experienced from my mother caused me to live most of my childhood afraid. Whenever I found myself within arm's reach of my mother, I would flinch and cover up for fear of being hit, even if I hadn't done anything wrong. The fact that I was constantly being put down caused me to believe I would never amount to much. I spent most of my teenage years doing just enough to get by, not realizing that while I was getting by, my life was going by.

I made a habit of missing school regularly. Only on rare occasions would I make it through an entire week without an absence. This was my way of rebelling against my mother. I didn't realize that I was hurting myself a lot more than I was hurting her.

The bigger I got, the older I got, the more confident I became. The more confidence I gained, the more I would stand up against my mother. My newfound confidence almost cost me my life. I will never forget that cold winter night that changed my life.

It was around eleven o'clock at night when my mother walked in the house. My father, who was the one I depended on for protection, was away on a business trip. That meant the only one who could protect me, was me.

My mother was upset to find my fourteen-year-old sister and me still awake. I can still hear her fiery voice, "Get the extension cord and get in here. You both are getting a beating. " I was seventeen, and I refused to let anyone attack me, including my mother. Instead of coming into the room where she was waiting, I grabbed my coat and ran out of the house. She came to the window and asked me to please come back inside. She convinced me that she was really sorry and was not going to do anything, it was safe to come back in side. She calmly said to me, "I am sorry, I had a bad day and I overreacted."

I believed her, and once I got inside, she walked towards me. "You've been around your father too long," she said, and swung the extension cord, wrapping it around my arm. When I grabbed it from her, she reached for a two-by-four piece of wood and swung it at me. "She's trying to hurt me bad!" I thought. I somehow managed to dodge the board. It was moving so fast, I could hear the wind as it flew by me. It hit the wall and fell out of her hand. At that point, she grabbed a pair of large scissors and aimed for my side. At that point, the thought in my head changed to, "She's not just going to hurt me, *she's going to kill me*!" Fortunately, my uncle was staying with us at the time. He reached in and knocked her hand down just in time. She was only inches away from my ribcage.

I ran out of the house and remained gone for four days. There was no way that I was coming back until my father returned from his trip. I also missed school each of these days. When my father returned, a fight broke out between my parents over what had happened. My father packed his things and moved to California, a long way from our home in Maywood, a small Chicago suburb. I was devastated.

I have to say I believe much of what my mother did was a result of her drug habit. It was not unusual to see her and her friends get high. It was not unusual, but each time I saw it, it hurt and angered me. I could never understand why I was subjected to such a life. I couldn't understand why my mother felt the need to use drugs. The fact that I never felt loved by my mother caused me to have very low self-esteem. Why didn't she love me? I continued asking this question to myself for years.

My focus was now on everything but school. I managed to finish my senior year, but because of all of my absences, I had to attend summer school before I received my diploma. Upon graduating, I worked in a small factory, making a little money for a lot of work. It didn't take me long to realize that it was not for me. I did what I thought was the only answer. I joined the United States Air Force. Once again, I was at a place I didn't want to be.

While I will acknowledge that the Air Force did me more good than harm, I just couldn't conform to their way of life. I spent my entire childhood being bullied and ordered around, and here it was happening again. As I reflect back, it is increasingly obvious that God's will sometimes sends us down some challenging roads before we reach our destination.

Just before joining the Air Force, I began boxing. I fell in love with the sport and had dreams of turning pro someday. I continued boxing while in the military, and was doing very well until my worst nightmare came true. I was fighting for the Southern California amateur championship. Late in the fifth round, I threw a punch and SNAP went my shoulder. My trainer realized I was in trouble, and wisely stopped the fight. It was a career ending injury. Again, I felt that all-too-familiar sense of devastation. I had poured everything I had into boxing, and now it was over.

Shortly after I injured my shoulder, I was discharged from the Air Force. I returned home to Chicago, only to discover I had no home, no job, no car, no money, no education beyond high school, and worst of all I had no plan! After spending the first few months sleeping wherever I could, my father's sister opened her doors to me. She looked at me and challenged me to stand up and take control of my life. As though she was my guardian angel, she spoke into my life with words that ignited my spirit. "Your past does not have to equal your future," she said. "This is your life and you have the ability to be whatever you want t be".

Her concern and love for me was something I never experienced from my mother. I stopped believing the lie my mother told me for so many years that I would never amount to much. For the first time in my life, I felt like someone could see potential in me that even I couldn't see. For the first time in my life, I felt like someone really believed in me. She inspired me to stand up again. Just like a boxer who was knocked down after receiving a blow, I was on the mat. I had to make a decision whether I was going to get up and keep fighting or stay down for the count. She encouraged me to let go of my past. She challenged me to do what no one in my family had done, graduate from college.

I got a job and worked full-time during the day, and went to school at night. I was a man on a mission. I refused to see myself as anything but a success. I refused to accept the opinions of others who were so sure I would amount to nothing. I refused to be defeated.

My goal in boxing was to be a champion. When I was injured and my career ended, I felt that my dream of being a champion ended along with it. What I didn't realize then was that you don't have to be an athlete to be a champion. It took me eight long, and very trying years to graduate, but when I looked over and saw the proud expressions on the faces of my aunt, my father and my wife, I realized that I had become the very thing I dreamed of being, a champion. Not a boxing champion, but a champion of life!

Pounding the Pavement
By Troy Stende

Have you ever had a time in your life when you said yes to everything and were way too busy? This was about a time in my life that I questioned how smart I was about the choices I made.

I was a student at San Jose State University, in California. During one semester I did it all- and then some. I was a Division 1 gymnast, pledged a fraternity, maintained a social life, took time to write and call home, washed my own clothes, cooked my own meals (one of the down sides of living off campus), and financially supported myself.

I had a job as a security guard at a blood, urine and stool laboratory. That's right, it was my job to guard the crap! I am neither big, nor aggressive, and to look at me you might laugh out loud to think I was a security guard. I did all this, and I had no idea what I had gotten myself into.

This was a typical week of my life: I'd wake up Sunday night and go to work at 1:30A.M. I'd work until 8:00 A.M. Right from work, I'd dash to classes all day. Of course the classes that I needed were only available at 8:00A.M. —it's the law, isn't it? Then I'd grab a quick bite to eat and race off to gymnastics practice and work out for four hours, flipping all over the place, flying through the air (with the greatest of ease), and finishing with an exhausting strength workout at the end.

Monday night was fraternity-meeting night. We, the pledges, would meet for a couple hours, and then go to the big meeting with all the actives. I can't tell you about what we did at those meetings (I could tell you, but then I'd have to kill you), but I can tell you that I never fell asleep during one. After all that fun stuff I'd go study, if I had time. Finally it was bedtime, but I only slept for two hours, because I had to go to work again from 1:30A.M. until 8:00A.M. (I'm getting tired just remembering this).

Luckily, Tuesday morning I didn't have class so I could sleep- wahoo!!! However, I could only sleep for a couple of hours because I had to get to practice. Whether you're an athlete or not, you can imagine how hard it is working out when you're sleep deprived. After many hours of intense workout I would eat dinner and then back to work again-this time for the early shift, at 8:00 P.M. (Are you keeping up with me?) I'd work until 1:30 A.M. and finally I'd get to sleep—well, it was more like a short nap because I had class at 8:00A.M. So I'd repeat the cycle again where I'd go to class all day, and right to another grueling practice, and *finally* on Thursday night, I had time to get some bona fide sleep (unless of course, I had to travel to a gymnastics meet). Once I laid my head down, I would sleep for about two days!

When I look back at what I did, I can't believe I got through it. I did all that?! Not only did I get through it, I excelled. There were so many times that I wanted to give up, but for some reason I didn't. Something inside of me just kept my feet moving- one foot in front of the other- one step at a time. Maybe it was my desire to succeed, or I just didn't know any better, but I think that it all came down to my inner drive. I knew that this was what I had signed up for and I was going to see it through. But I also knew that I would have dropped certain things if my health, personal relationships, grades, or happiness had been suffering. I still believe that when any of those things start happening, a line has been crossed and something needs to change.

What got me through was strong drive, but it didn't seem like that when I was in the middle of it. To me, it was just getting up and doing what I had to do. When I was doing it, it was like, "Big deal, whatever. Of course this is what I do. How could I do it any differently?" The interesting thing was when the next year came around, and I wasn't nearly as busy, my grades weren't as good, and I was about half as productive. I later learned from a study that students do better when they have a job and work at least 20 hours a week. If they work less than that, they have lower grades. Regardless of whether the study is true or not, what I know is that when I am super busy, I am forced to prioritize my time. I become far more efficient and productive. My life is much more fulfilling because I am achieving my goals and living with purpose.

For my tireless efforts, not only did I become a full-fledged fraternity brother, I also received the Academic All-American Award! This is an award given to student athletes having over a 3.5 GPA and excelling in his/her sport. Of all the awards I've received in my life, this is the one I am most proud of. I learned then that with perseverance, hard work, and direction, I can achieve things that may seem overwhelming- and I can receive benefits I never could have imagined!

So when you feel yourself feeling overwhelmed, sit down and imagine all the great stuff that will be yours when you make it through that hectic time in your life. The rewards can be incredible.

Daddy's Little Girl
By Yolande Chatman

By my 21st birthday, I will have seen and been through so much. To be able to overcome and withstand it all has been a blessing. The most troubling part of my life was the father-daughter relationship (and I use the word "relationship" loosely) between my father, stepfather, and me. I have always wondered what a "real" father-daughter relationship should be like. I have always wanted to be a "daddy's girl," one who gets that extra $75 from her father to buy that perfect, although more expensive prom dress; one who does no wrong in her father's eyes. Growing up, I would ask myself, "What happened? Did I do something wrong? Why are my cousins laughing with their fathers at the family gatherings? Why is my best friend having lunch with her father after church?" I saw other people's dads as the epitome of fatherhood. Maybe they could teach a course on how to be a good daddy. I would be the first to pre-register my father and stepfather.

I was involved in quite a few activities while in school such as the orchestra, choir, and cheerleading. When I had a performance, neither of my fathers would show. My mom would always try to make it up to me by buying me something nice or taking me out to dinner. This was her way of trying to make me feel better. Ironically, when I would do something great like make the honor roll or win a scholarship, they were the first to say, "That's my daughter!" Really? How much credit should they be taking?

Fortunately, I could always talk to my mom about how I felt about my fathers. Because she could see my disappointment, she always took the blame. One day, she told me, "Baby, it's my fault for putting you in this position. If I ever thought that this would create such a problem, I never would have remarried." She did and said everything that she could to keep me from resenting the constant letdowns from the men in my life.

As I grew older, I realized just how much a true father-daughter relationship was missing in my life. Actually, I had an abundance of meaningful relationships, but I neglected to utilize them because of my concentration on the void left by my two fathers. For example, when a person loses his sight, his hearing becomes keener. This same principle applied to my life. My relationship with my fathers was weak, but other things in my life became subsequently stronger. My grades, my family relationships, and most of all, my walk with God have become focal points in my life. I never realized that I already had the type of relationship that I was longing for. I was just looking in the wrong place for it. It was like looking for some money in a college student's bank account, it just wasn't there.

I now know that I was, am, and will forever be a "daddy's girl." My Heavenly Father has assured me of this. Instead of being given more money for a prom dress, God has given me joy and peace in my life. However, unlike the prom dress, it is something that people will see more than once. I no longer search for things or people to fill "the God spot" in my life. I have learned that all I needed to do was listen to God when He speaks and have the courage to do what He tells me to do. Everything else will fall into place. When I stopped making demands and started asking questions, my relationship with Him blossomed.

God had to break me down in order for me to understand what He actually had in store for me. I had to truly see that I was focusing on the wrong things in life. He showed me I controlled my thoughts and emotions. Furthermore, I was only responsible for my actions, not how others acted toward me. I released myself from responsibility for my fathers' actions. And best of all, I already possessed everything that I wanted. As the expression says, "My blessings already were." As I matured and changed *my* perspective of life, love, and relationships, I no longer felt incomplete.

The quest for a sense of wholeness has been the biggest struggle in my life. Though my earthly fathers may have let me down, I know that I can always enjoy the comfort of having a Heavenly Father that has been there with me all along. Though I acknowledge that I still have work to do, through my relationship with Him, I have found many of the missing pieces to the puzzle. I am Yolande Suzanne Chatman, Daddy's little girl.

About the Authors

Cheronda Simmons resides in Austin Texas. She received her Bachelor degree in Business Administration with a concentration in Management of Information Systems from the University of Houston. She earned her MBA in e-Commerce at St. Edward's University. Cheronda is a member of Toastmasters International and Women in Technology International (WITIT). In her spare time, she enjoys volunteering at her church. Cheronda currently works for Dell Computer Corporation as a Quality Assurance Analyst. Her work has allowed her to create processes that make organizations operate more efficiently.

Jacqueline W. Ivey is a native of Kingstree, South Carolina, is Director of Educational Talent Search, a federally-funded TRIO program serving first-generation college individuals, at York Technical College. Jacqueline earned a Bachelor of Arts degree in History from Winthrop College in 1991 and a Master of Arts degree in Human Resource Development from Webster University in 2001. An advocate for youth, Jacqueline is very passionate about programs serving "at-risk", "disadvantaged" populations, having been labeled as such in her youth. Her affiliations as a member of the Catawba Regional Workforce Investment Area Youth Council; a former Executive Board member of the Williamsburg Branch of Parents Anonymous of South Carolina and the Williamsburg County Tech Prep Consortium are a testament to that dedication of leveling the playing field for the targeted population. Jacqueline may be contacted at (803) 981-7160 or (866) 277-3003.

Jason Gipson is a native of Houston, Texas. He is a graduate of the University of Texas at Austin with a BS in mechanical engineering and a BA in Spanish. He has worked as a Senior Consultant with a Texas-based software development company. At the time of this publication, Jason is preparing for service in the Dominican Republic as a Peace Corps volunteer. Jason can be reached at jgip@alumni.utexas.net.

Johnny Campbell is the president and founder of Speak On IT, a company that helps individuals and corporations mentally condition themselves to change in order to achieve the personal and financial success they desire. He is an expert on Transition, Organizational Change, and Motivation. Johnny has combined his passion for training with an entertaining speaking style to create presentations that are inspiring, deep in content and entertaining. Based on his experiences gained from being a survivor of multiple corporate downsizings and mergers, he has become "The Transition Man." Currently, Johnny travels the country showing individuals how they can overcome the personal and professional obstacles created by change to become a winner. The message Johnny shares captivates audiences with its inspiring tone, entertaining format and practical uses.

Jowanda Durham graduated with a bachelor's of fine arts in drama from the University of Georgia. After college, she interned at DownSouth Filmworks Inc., an independent film company. She has completed two screenplays and placed as a semi-finalist in The Chesterfield Writing Competition for Amblin Entertainment. Jowanda continues to write, act, and direct locally today. She is currently writing a novel entitled , *SCAR* and developing a web-based business. She worked at Middle Georgia College in Student Activities. Jowanda can be reached at (866) 554-7219.

Dr. Kevin D. Rome resides in Indianapolis, Indiana. He was born in Columbus, Georgia. He received his Bachelor's of Arts Degree from Morehouse College and his Master's of Education degree from the University of Georgia. Additionally, he received his Ph.D. from the University of Texas-Austin in the area of Educational Administration. He also served as Assistant Dean of Students at the University of Texas for five years. Prior to that time he worked at California Polytechnic State University in San Luis Obispo, California. Presently, he serves as the Assistant Vice Chancellor for Student Life and Diversity at Indiana University-Purdue University at Indianapolis (IUPUI). Kevin is the co-owner of "2 Care Unlimited" (www.2cusaab.org), a Ohio-based consulting firm specializing in human development needs of clients around the country as well as internationally. He is happily married and enjoys traveling, watching college football, writing poetry, meeting people, and working with diversity initiatives around the country. Kevin can be reached at (317) 274-8990.

Kim Crayton- It is Kim's intention to aid people in living more conscious lives by helping them develop the decision-making skills they need to manage their lives effectively. People are struggling to make sense of a world that often times makes no sense and they are attempting to do this without the aid of an internal compass. Kim is the founder of Healthy Choice Healthy Lives, an organization that "helps people understand that they have choices." In Kim's own words, "One must understand that you have choices and that it is in choosing that you will discover who and what you are. Merely surviving your life is not your soul's desire; only in success will your soul find itself rejoicing. " For more on Kim, please visit www.healthychoiceshealthylives.com. Kim can be reached at kmcrayton1@msn.com.

Kirk Nugent-Hard hitting, poignant and thought provoking, this 1999 Nuyorican Poets Cafe Grand Slam Champion is a spoken word icon. Born and raised in Kingston, Jamaica, Kirk Nugent affectionately known as, "America's #1 Motivational Poet", migrated to the United States in 1983. Nugent has been performing poetry throughout the United States and Canada for three years. In 1999 he was featured in CBS "60 Minutes" television special covering slam poetry. The

People's Poet has performed on college campuses from Texas to Toronto, Main to Miami, Chicage to Cali. Kirk has opened for the Queen Latifah Show as well as shared the stage with Reverend Al Sharpton and Attorney Alton Maddox. He was the Captain of the 1999 Nuyorican National Slam Team. Currently, he is the coach of the 2000 Nuyorican Slam Team. Kirk is a visionary and definitely on of the hardest working poets in the Northeastern region of the U.S. He recently released his first spoken word CD entitled, "The Unpopular Truth." Kirk can be reached at kirkdpoet@aol.com or www.ironicworld.com.

Lawana Gladney, Ph.D- Formerly an elementary school, middle school, and college professor, she has developed many programs, which include, cognition, motivation, classroom management, leadership, motivation, diversity, communication, stress management, and others. As author of The Five Keys to "REALL" Control, Going beyond a Discipline Plan, Dr. Gladney has revolutionized classroom management. Dr. Gladney has traveled throughout the country speaking to various audiences. Her extensive years of research in the field of motivation coupled with her energetic presentation style leaves audiences ready to move, shake, or step aside. Lawana is actively involved in many community and church activities. She is constantly on the move, balancing work and the lives of her four children. She currently resides in Dallas, Texas with her husband, Charles, and children, Jordan, Bria, Jaslynne, and Alexia. For more on Lawana, please visit her website at www.drgladney.com.

Lee Howard currently resides in Texas with his wife, Shea. He is now a realtor for a small firm and in his spare time he practices his artwork and plays basketball. Lee can be contacted Lee_M_Howard@hotmail.com.

Manuel Diotte- Change and adversity are no strangers to Manuel. With only six months to live at the age of seven, our featured speaker is a walking miracle.   Having had over thirty operations, two years of chemotherapy, and several months of radiation treatment, Manuel overcame insurmountable odds. In 1987 at the tender age of 18, he overcame the hurdle of his youth to become the youngest Realtor in the State of Texas with sales in the millions worth of real estate. Today, he is an entrepreneur, professional speaker, trainer, consultant and the author of the hit book, *Happiness is a Pair of Shorts!*, and a contributing author to the New York Best Seller *Chicken Soup for the Surviving Soul*. Manuel has spoken to over three million people on the radio, has appeared on television with two million viewers, and conducted numerous seminars with thousands in attendance, Manuel helps individuals and companies achieve greatness by dealing with change and coping with adversity. For more on Manuel, please visit www.manueldiotte.com.

Marcel Brunel is currently a Senior Managing Performance Consultant with Acclivus Corporation. He is a business advisor to some of Acclivus' most prestigious clients, including Dell, Energizer, Kraft, and FedEx. A former Airborne Ranger with the US Army, Marcel hasn't watched television at home since December 1997. He travels so much that when he's in town, he cherishes quality time with his wife and two children. Before coming to Acclivus, Marcel was a sales rep at Dictaphone, where he was the top national sales producer in 1994. Marcel graduated in 1992 with a bachelor's degree in child psychology from Texas A&M University. Marcel can be reached at Marcel.Brunel@acclivus.com or (972) 385-1277.

Sanyika Calloway Boyce earned her B.S. from Norfolk State University. She founded SCB Enterprise in 1997 and the debut of the Financial Fitness Institute is scheduled for late fall 2003. Praised as "The #1 Financial Fitness Coach For College Students" and passionate about advancing the cause to "Spread Financial Literacy One Person At A Time", Sanyika speaks to thousands of high school and college students nationwide. For more on Sanyika, please visit her website at www.4dacode.com. Sanyika can be contacted via email at Sanyika@4dacode.com.

Sean Stephenson-Born with a rare bone disorder, Stephenson wasn't expected to live through the first night. But he did. Sean has accomplished more than most people twice his age, and he's done it against the odds and from a wheelchair. In 1998, Sean was publicly recognized by President Bill Clinton and has testified before the United States Senate. From serving as the Spokesperson for the Osteogenesis Imperfecta Foundation to appearing on CNN and featured in *The New York Times*, he is living proof dreams can become realities through perseverance, positive thinking and a get-it-done attitude. Sean is the author of *How YOUth Can Succeed!* It is more than a book; it is a tool for individuals to recognize their full-potential and empower them to reach their goals, even in the face of adversity. For more information about Sean's presentations or his book, call (708) 482-3128 or visit Sean on the web at: www.seanstephenson.com.

Sean Michael Watkins is a junior at the University of Texas at Austin. He is double-majoring in History and African-American Studies, with the intention to pursue a PhD in African-American Studies and attend law school. In his extracurricular activities, Sean faithfully serves as Spiritual Development Chair in Student African American Brotherhood, and Small Group Bible Study Leader for Texas Gospel Fellowship. He proudly hails from Houston, Texas. Sean can be reached at sean2282@hotmail.com.

Sporty King is an expert on personal success, the impact of words on our lives, and a master at turning any negative into a positive. This 18-year veteran of *The Wall Street Journal* rose from a messenger to an Advertising Sales Manager before retiring to pursue his oratorical gift. He is a creative, dynamic speaker with 25+ years of corporate and entrepreneurial expertise who appeals to audiences of all ages, sizes, ethnicities and genders. When you remember to hire Sporty to speak with your people, they won't have to remember him from somewhere else. Sporty can be contacted at 708-366-1445 or Spoetry@aol.com.

Tiffany M. Pertillar is a senior Human Services major at Geneva College. She intends to graduate in May of 2003. Upon graduation, she will be entering law school to obtain a dual MSW/Juris Doctorate degree. She has spoken several times to young girls about her own teenage experiences, and hopes to continue this in the future. Tiffany can be contacted at Mydestiny07@hotmail.com or (717)-657-3219.

Tony Magee is a native son of South Central Los Angeles. He is a graduate of Westchester High School and holds a Bachelor of Science degree in Industrial Engineering from Cal State Northridge. During his graduate trek, Tony became the first African-American to graduate with a Master of Science (M.S.) degree in Materials Science & Engineering from Lehigh University. He earned an M.B.A. from Pepperdine University. Tony completed Executive M.B.A. studies in Global Enterprise Management, Policies, Organizations and Economics from Kellogg College at Oxford University in England. Tony is President of PlatinumStar Performance Systems a professional and personal development firm, and author of Can't Stuff a Great Life into a Small Dream! He is a Professional Member of the National Speakers Association Tony's main philosophy in life is "you are what you think about, all day long." For more on Tony, please visit www.platinumstar.com. Tony can be reached at tony@platinumstar.com.

Tony Powell- Tony Powell is the Heavyweight Champion of Success who helps your organization see the opportunity in every challenge, and view every setback as a setup for a comeback. Tony is an award winning motivational speaker who has been firing up audiences for over 15 years. Tony speaks from the heart sharing his incredible life experiences to inspire, educate, and encourage. Tony is living proof that with positive thinking, determination, and action, you can overcome any obstacle and achieve any goal. For more on Tony, please visit www.successchampion.com. Tony can be reached at powellgoodlife@aol.com or (630) 778-2270.

Troy Stende- A professional keynote speaker and high-impact trainer, Troy Stende is considered one of the best young speakers/trainers on the college circuit. Troy has addressed audiences in over 30 states across the country and around the world, including Singapore and Hong Kong. For seven years, Troy has been a facilitator for the country's premiere accelerated learning programs, and conducts life-changing leadership, communication, and relationship workshops. Troy is a contributor to such books as *Major in Success*, by Patrick Combs, and *The Backdoor Guide to Short-Term Job Adventures*, by Michael Landes. During college he was a Kappa Sigma Fraternity member and a NCAA Division 1 gymnast. Troy also appeared on National Public Radio, and was featured in Campus Activities Today, and USA Today for living his dreams. Most recently, Troy was awarded, 2002 Best Campus Speaker, from the Association for the Promotion of Campus Activities. Troy can be reached at 1-866-2STENDE or www.troystende.com.

Yolande Suzanne Chatman is currently a junior biology/pre-pharmacy major at Baylor University. She is active member of Baylor's gospel choir, Heavenly Voices. Yolande also enjoys volunteering at Methodist Children's Home as a Lifesaver Volunteer and recruiting for the Baylor football team. Yolande can be reached at gotchago@netscapenet.

Jonathan Sprinkles is a rare gem. Still in his twenties, he is the owner of two successful businesses, Sprinklisms and Instruments of Peace. Sprinklisms is a personal development company that "teaches beautiful people to act like it". Instruments of Peace is the publishing company that produced his two books, *Why Settle? Be the Best YOU That YOU Can Be* and *Student Success Stories.* Jonathan has been featured in *Youth Today Magazine* for his work with young adults and *Campus Activities Magazine* for being one of the hottest speakers in the college market. His article on leadership, "What to do With Your Faithful Few" was also featured in Toastmasters International's magazine.

A University of Texas at Austin graduate, Jonathan was a three-time honoree of the African American Culture Committee's Top 10 Most Upstanding Men award. For his commitment to the UT community, he was also distinguished as the Barbara Jordan Leadership Award Recipient and received membership into the Dean's Dozen, a group of twelve student leaders hand-picked by the university's Dean of Students out of an enrollment of over 50,000 students.

Jonathan currently speaks into the lives of thousands of students and adults annually across the country. Earning the distinction of "Advanced Toastmaster" in Toastmasters International, he has won the title of District in speech evaluation--one of 71 in the world. Jonathan pours the same spirit into the series of high-energy presentations. His messages seek to entertain, educate and edify. Jonathan delivers results, not rhetoric.

Success Story Writing Guide

Have you learned any valuable lessons lately? Have you endured tough times? If the answer is yes to either of these questions, **you have a success story!**

We will show you how to quickly turn your everyday experiences into a masterfully crafted story. Before we get started, there are a few things that you have to do:

1. Go to a comfortable or familiar place where you can be relaxed and free from distractions.
2. Relax your body and open your mind. Release the stress and tension from the day. A cluttered mind is not a creative mind.
3. Say to yourself, "I have a great story within me that I must tell. I am going to help others by sharing my experiences. I will recall every detail as if it was yesterday. I have it all inside of me."
4. Decide that you are going to see yourself through the entire story-writing process, come what may. Promise yourself that you will not stop until you have completely finished the project.
5. See the entire story being played out in your mind. See the colors, hear the people, feel the emotions — relive the event!

Now that you have an open mind that is ready work for you, transferring it to paper will be easy. Grab a piece of paper or a notebook and begin to write down every detail that you can remember. Don't worry about it making sense yet. Write in the margins, write upside down, draw pictures. Do what you have to do—just write!

Lesson learned: _____

_____

_____

How did I learn this lesson?_____

_____

_____

_____

_____

_____

_____

_____

_____

What was I like before the experience? _____

_____

_____

_____

_____

_____

_____

_____

What was I like during the experience? _____
_____
_____
_____
_____
_____

How did I change after the experience? _____
_____
_____
_____
_____
_____

What would life be like had I failed or did not learn this lesson? _____
_____
_____
_____
_____

Key Characters:
A _____ B_____ C _____ D_____

Were there any important one-liners, dialogue, or words of wisdom that helped you out? _____
_____
_____
_____
_____
_____
_____

Trust me, you now have everything that you need to create the best story that has ever been told. Actually, it's probably a lot easier than you ever thought. Just put it all together, let someone read it, revise it a couple of times and you're done!

There are a few things that you must make sure to include before you complete your project. Few good stories go without them.

The 6 Key Components Of A Knee-Slappin', Gut-Bustin', Tear-Jerkin', "Girl, No He *Didn't!*" Good Story

1. A definite beginning, middle and conclusion.
2. A sense of "what's at stake" if you were to fail. Why should the reader care? Why is the event significant?
3. A clear message. What's the point of the story?
4. Dialogue—characters speaking to each other, or an internal dialogue within your mind. This adds texture to the story and let's the reader see life through your perspective.
5. Vivid descriptions of the events. People are audio, visual or kinesthetic (action) learners. You have to appeal to each personality type to capture your entire audience. What did it look like? What did she sound like? How did it move?
6. A title that appropriately ties in with the story. Don't give away too much, but don't be too vague.

Give yourself plenty of time to get it to look exactly the way that you want it to. As one writer said, "There are no great writers, only great rewriters."

SPEAKING ENGAGEMENTS

Many of the Student Success Stories authors are available for speaking engagements. Please feel free to contact us for information and availability.

WRITE TO US!

Nothing would please us more than to know that our stories have positively impacted other people. If you have been moved by one of the stories please write us and let us know.

If you have a Success Story of your own,
please submit it via email to Jonathan Sprinkles at
Jonathan@Sprnklisms.com
Re: Success Story.
All submissions must be no longer than 1,500 words.

BULK PURCHASE DISCOUNTS

This book is available for bulk purchase discounts. If you are interested in buying *Student Success Stories i*n large quantities, please email us at:
Sales@Sprnklisms.com
Re: Bulk Purchase